Take
Another
Step

ANDREW HILL

Published by Crossbridge Books
Worcester
www.crossbridgeeducational.com

ISBN 978 0 9569089 3 3

British Library Cataloguing in Publication Data
A catalogue record for this book is available from the British Library

First published in Great Britain by Andrew Hill Ministries 2019
Copyright © 2019 Andrew L Hill

To

My three Fathers

My earthly father Alfred Hill who was amazingly
loving and wise

To my spiritual father John Bedford who
believed in me and provided opportunity

To my heavenly Father whose abundance of
love and grace has got me this far

Thank you

Contents

Appreciation

Andrew is a breed of Christian teacher who understands the heart of our faith - the person of Jesus, the kingdom of God, the plan of salvation. In 'Take Another Step', he applies his gifts to laying out for us the message of the Beatitudes with great skill. This book is a breath of fresh air! Nothing stuffy or religious here. Instead, his work is full of insightful revelation and practical application, taking us on a journey of the heart to experience God's plan for our lives. I thoroughly recommend 'Take Another Step.'

Tony Wastall, author, Principal of LifeSpring School of Ministry and LifeSpring Global, Wolverhampton

Acknowledgements

My grateful thanks to my good friends Rev. Linda Crebbin and Dave Sharrock who took the time to read the manuscript and provide me with suggestions for additions and amendments that have greatly enhanced the text and layout, and to the many friends who have persevered with, cajoled, and encouraged me over the last few years, and have given me the impetus to keep going, particularly my sister, Janie, who has always believed in me.

Thank you also to those who have kindly written an appreciation.

Thank you to the late John Bedford for the 'self-....' words used for each of the Beatitudes that are taken from his teaching.

And finally, many thanks go to Ruth Price-Mohr of Crossbridge Books for her help, guidance, and input, in finally bringing this book to publication.

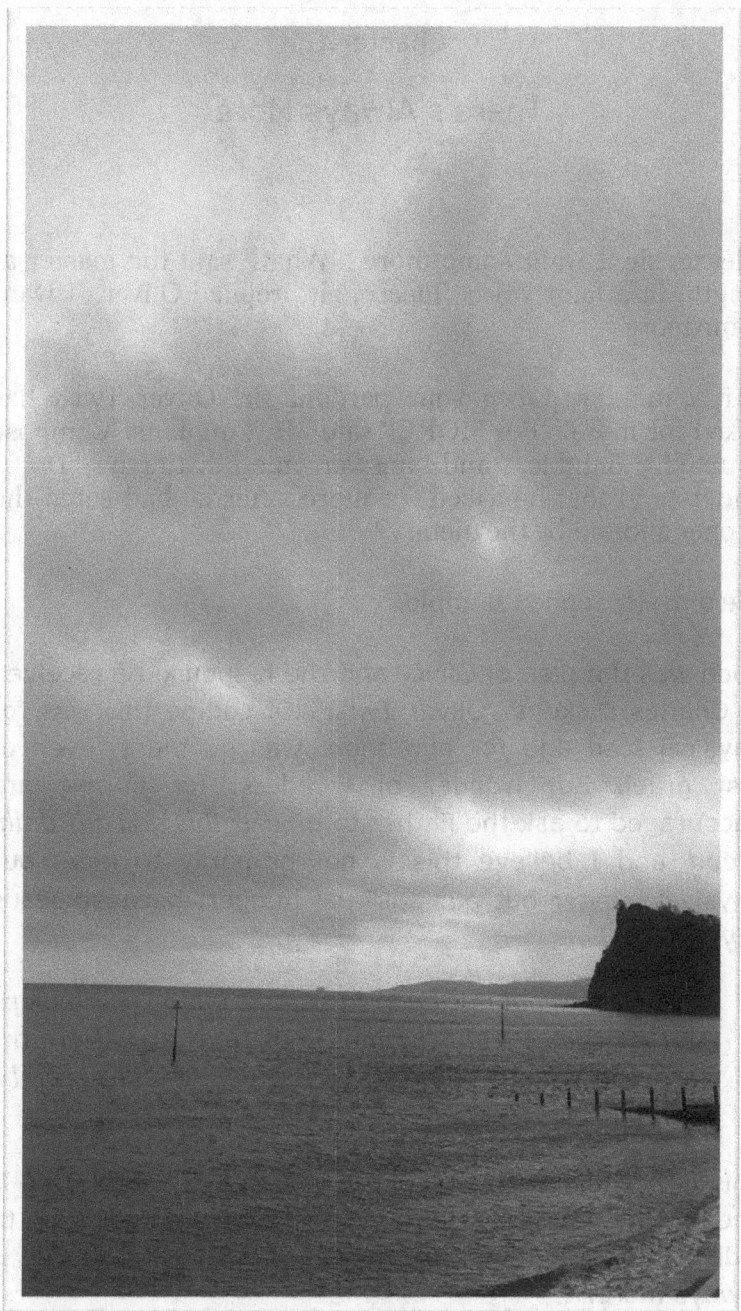

Chapter 1

There's Always More

'Please, sir, I want some more.' 'What!' said the master at length, in a faint voice. 'Please, sir,' replied Oliver, 'I want some more.'

'Mr. Limbkins, I beg your pardon, sir! Oliver Twist has asked for more!' 'For MORE!' said Mr. Limbkins. 'Compose yourself, Bumble, and answer me distinctly. Do I understand that he asked for more, after he had eaten the supper allotted by the dietary?'

'He did, sir,' replied Bumble.

Such was the plea of Oliver and the response he received in Charles Dickens' 'Oliver Twist'. Of course this was for physical food and for him there was no more, even of just gruel. But wonder of wonders, for us we are encouraged to ask the Father to *give us this day our daily bread[1]* and I believe this is not primarily to meet our physical hunger but our spiritual hunger, because Jesus says to us,

> *One does not live by bread alone, but by every word that comes from the mouth of God[2]* and *'I am the bread of life. Whoever comes to me will never be hungry.[3]*

This is because with God there is ALWAYS more! This is one of my favourite statements, to congregations, to individuals, and even to myself – with God there is always more.

4

I remember swimming in the sea and thinking how well the sea represents the Father. I can experience Him in a multitude of ways. I can be energetic or relaxed, I can swim or paddle, stay in the shallows, or go in the deep water, I can go to the left or the right, or be noisy or quiet. My experience of Father is endless, and tomorrow I can go further, deeper; explore something different.

In Him we live and move and have our being.[4]

With Father there is always more!

When I was in my mid-teens, I was struggling to work out how growth in the Christian life actually worked, so I went to an adult teacher in the Sunday school and asked the question. "What steps should I take to progress as a Christian; how does it actually work in practice?" I was told that after becoming a Christian, and making a commitment to Christ Jesus, a person then got baptised in water and then baptised in the Holy Spirit. I said, "That's it?" The answer was "Yes, that's the Christian life." Even at age fifteen I knew there had to be more to it than that and that I must have received at best the short version of an over-simplification! This book tries to answer my own question of long ago using the Beatitudes as the basis for the steps to take. So if you want to go on in your Christian faith and want to know the next step, this book is for you. Remember, with God there is always more.

Before we start, I should also mention that I have used several different expressions to refer to God the Father. These are intended to be interchangeable and the use in any particular place is not intended to signify anything except my preferred expression at that point. Now there are some questions on the next page for you to ponder.

Jot down your thoughts and responses to these questions
then see if your answers change as you continue to read.

KEY QUESTIONS

1. What do you think it means to be blessed?

2. What does it mean to be poor in spirit?

3. Should you give up your self-sufficiency?

4. Do you mourn for your sins?

5. Are you characterised by self-confidence?

6. Do you think the world revolves around you?

7. Why was Jesus described as meek?

8. Do you feel self-fulfilled?

9. How hungry are you for God?

10. Judgmental v Merciful, where do you score?

11. What is self-gratification?

12. What do you understand by purity?

13. Does self-consciousness overcome obedience?

14. What does it mean to be a peacemaker?

15. Are you ready for persecution?

There are a number of prayers throughout the book and I encourage you to pray the prayers and enlarge and add to them as much as you can.

A Prayer

Father, my desire is to go on in my relationship with you; to build day-by-day; to know you more; that I may decrease and you may increase in my life. Thank you that your Holy Spirit is at work in me to cause me to want what you want and do what you do. Help me through reading this book for this to become an increasing reality in my life.

Amen

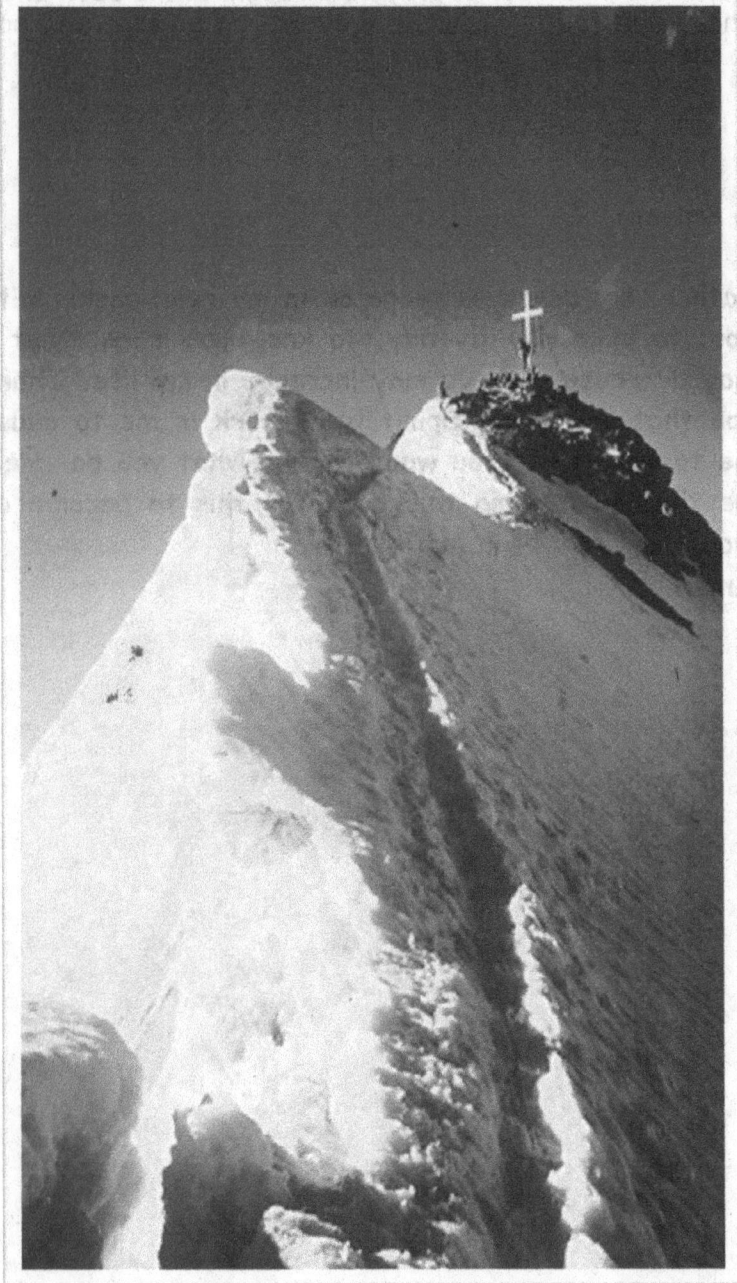

Chapter 2

The Beatitudes

The Beatitudes! What a great subject! These are the first words of Jesus' first major discourse as recorded by Matthew in his gospel. What could be better?

But I had a problem and I wonder if this will resonate with you?

The Beatitudes were fairly well known to me and together with the Lord's Prayer were possibly some of the most well-known words spoken by Jesus. I had heard the Beatitudes preached on numerous occasions and I took the view that mostly everything that needed to be said had already been said. The Beatitudes were really 'old hat' and basic, and it was time to move on. Despite this, I admit that in reality, for most of my life, I had only been able to quote possibly six out of the eight Beatitudes at any one time, not necessarily the same six on each occasion, and certainly in no particular order, and even now I cannot recall hearing any teaching that produced any connection between the Beatitudes. They were simply a set of really good conditional promises that gave good insight into what clearly pleased Father God and invoked His blessing. They provided encouragement to seek Him, but no more.

I was asked to preach a series on the Beatitudes, to which my first reaction was, "O No!" based on the assumptions given above. However, preparation began. I read the Beatitudes in several versions of the Bible, read some commentaries to see if I could gain any inspiration, and then followed my usual practice of quietening my heart, committing it to Father, and meditating. I was surprised by my initial thoughts that were not in connection with the *individual* Beatitudes, but in connection with them as a *group*. Jesus spoke the Beatitudes at the beginning of the Sermon on the Mount and I wondered whether or not Jesus had been given a somewhat random list by the Holy Spirit as He spoke. Did I really believe that Father God was random in that sort of way? Did I really believe that Jesus, as He spoke the words He heard Father God saying, simply shared a list of unconnected promises?

As I pondered on these questions, I was more and more convinced that if Father God had spoken these words, then there was a reason behind the order in which they were spoken. This is very similar to the whole armour of God which again I believe is in an organised, incremental list.

But what was the reason? Why does being meek come later than being poor in spirit and why does being pure in heart follow being merciful?

What I discovered was that the Beatitudes set out a promise that if I give up more and more of myself, God will exchange more and more of His life to me. I discovered that the Beatitudes are cumulative or incremental (the process of increasing in number and extent), and they provide signposts for a journey that can be walked in blessing with Father God, building up spiritual maturity from beginning to end. It is no less than a blueprint for descending the hill of self and ascending the hill of the Lord; a lesson in discipleship for a life-time!

Here is a diagram of where we are going with the Beatitudes.

HILL of SELF   HILL of the LORD

H   Poor   Persecuted   E

U   X

M   Mourn   Peacemaker   A

B   L

L   Meek   Pure   T

E

⬇ Hunger   Merciful ⬆

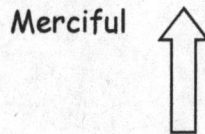

This book is not intended to be an exegesis of the text, but rather a practical explanation of each of the Beatitudes, and why it is where it is in the list. Some Beatitudes have a connection and lead more directly to

11

the next, but the over-riding understanding is to see them as a series of doorways, where one door has to be opened before the next can be reached. The emphasis is therefore on the first part of the Beatitude that states what is required from us, rather than on the reward that automatically follows in God's grace.

> *The Lord rewards everyone for His righteousness*
> *and His faithfulness[5]*
> *[God] rewards those who seek Him[6]*

I believe it will be a blessing to you in your journey with Father God and I know that for some of you it will be life changing.

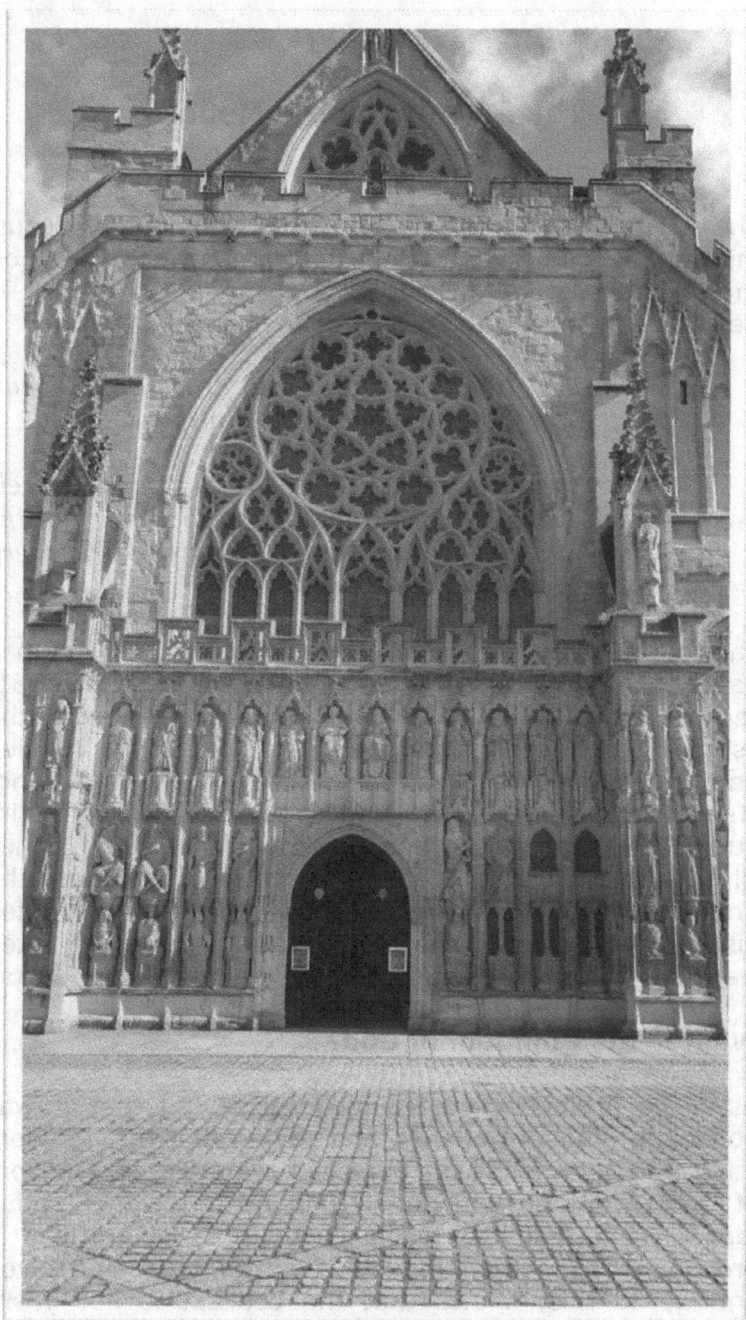

Chapter 3

The Sermon on the Mount

The Beatitudes come right at the beginning of Jesus' ministry in what is popularly known as the Sermon on the Mount recorded in Matthew's gospel in chapters 5-7. Before this, Matthew only records in chapter 4 that,

> *From that time Jesus began to proclaim, 'Repent, for the kingdom of heaven has come near*[7], and

> *Jesus went throughout Galilee, teaching in their synagogues and proclaiming the good news of the kingdom and curing every disease and every sickness among the people*[8].

Part of the teaching in the synagogue referred to may have been the reading and commentary on Isaiah 61, recorded in Luke chapter 4, where Jesus tells the listeners that Isaiah's prophecy is about to be fulfilled and their response was one of bewilderment asking, "Isn't this Joseph's son?" and eventually throwing Him out of the synagogue, and the town and trying to kill Him. Good start! But whichever of these records was the first in time, the first words of the first recorded discourse of Jesus to the crowds that gathered to listen were the Beatitudes. Let's look at some specifics aspects.

What is the Kingdom of God?

As Jesus prefaced His teaching by saying that it was about the Kingdom of God, and saying that the Kingdom had come, let us first ask ourselves, what is this Kingdom of God? What do you understand by this rather vague idea? The fact that Jesus gives multiple illustrations in order to explain the Kingdom, Matthew 13 being given entirely to this, shows that the concept is not easily grasped and to make it more difficult, the Bible refers to the Kingdom of God and the Kingdom of Heaven, but we should treat them as the same.

First, a kingdom of any kind is an area, usually geographical, that defines the place where a king or queen reigns. The United Kingdom is the area over which Queen Elizabeth II is acknowledged to be the reigning monarch. Her kingdom does not extend to France because her rule is not recognised there. But the Kingdom of God is not limited to any geographical area unless the whole world is regarded as this, but what it does indicate are the places where God's rule and reign is acknowledged, that is, God is the ruling authority. The Kingdom of Heaven is the place where God rules and reigns through His Son by the power of Holy Spirit.

Secondly, this is a spiritual kingdom not an earthly one. Jesus said to the Pharisees,

> *The kingdom of God does not come with observation; nor will they say, 'See here!' or 'See there!' For indeed, the kingdom of God is within you*[9].

What does this mean? Some translations use 'among you' but it is clear that the Kingdom is not an earthly kingdom but a spiritual kingdom with or among God's people and not something that can be visibly seen in a geographical way. No-one will be able to point to it but, although it is an invisible kingdom, it is none the less real.

Thirdly, as the Kingdom is right here among us, it must be on earth, and can therefore be experienced. When you move, the Kingdom moves with you so that it is wherever you are. This is why the disciples were taught to say, whether it was to those who accepted what they said or those who did not,

The Kingdom of God has come near.[10]

-o-o-o-o-

Does God want to bless you?

> *Then He began to speak, and taught them, saying:*
> *Blessed are the poor in spirit, for theirs is the*
> *kingdom of heaven. Blessed are those who mourn,*
> *for they will be comforted. Blessed are the meek, for*
> *they will inherit the earth. Blessed are those who*
> *hunger and thirst for righteousness, for they will be*
> *filled. Blessed are the merciful, for they will receive*
> *mercy. Blessed are the pure in heart, for they will*
> *see God. Blessed are the peacemakers, for they will*
> *be called children of God. Blessed are those who are*
> *persecuted for righteousness' sake, for theirs is the*
> *kingdom of heaven. Blessed are you when people*
> *revile you and persecute you and utter all kinds of*
> *evil against you falsely on my account. Rejoice and*
> *be glad, for your reward is great in heaven, for in*
> *the same way they persecuted the prophets who*
> *were before you[11].*

Now what did the crowd make of this teaching? Was it completely new to them? Did their Jewish understanding give them any insight into what Jesus was trying to say? The answer is, probably, yes, because they knew Torah and the prophets; what we call the Old Testament. Let's start at the beginning of the Old Testament and try to make the same connections they might have made. Let us think about the various verbs relating to God that are recorded in Genesis chapter 1: created, said, saw, separated, called, made, set, blessed, gave.

They are of course the verbs relating to creation, but the very first verb used to describe God's relationship with the people He had created was, 'blessed'. We see that God spoke first to the living creatures He had made,

16

> *God blessed them, saying, 'Be fruitful and multiply and fill the waters in the seas, and let birds multiply on the earth.*[12]

Then following this, God created man and woman in His own image and spoke to them.

> *God blessed them, and God said to them, 'Be fruitful and multiply, and fill the earth and subdue it*[13].

Surely it is significant that the very first direct communication Father God had with His creation was to bless them. In fact we find that bestowing blessing was quite a priority. One of the most often quoted passages is the well-known Aaronic blessing from Numbers.

> *The LORD bless you and keep you; the LORD make his face to shine upon you, and be gracious to you; the LORD lift up his countenance upon you, and give you peace.*[14]

This is an unfortunate translation because the original Hebrew inserts the word 'will' in every clause so that it should read, *"The Lord will bless you and keep you..."* etc. This then makes the rather less well-known following verse more understandable. That verse says,

> *So they shall put my name on the Israelites, and I will bless them*[15].

This is amazing because God is actually telling Moses and Aaron that if they say these words, if they invoke this blessing and prophesy it over the people, then God will perform it. It is no less than a full-scale delegation of authority to invoke God's blessing upon people. It must be very high on God's agenda. We find that this was endorsed by Jesus who when the disciples brought the children to Him,

17

He took them up in His arms, laid His hands on them, and blessed them [16].

Now the hearers of the Sermon on the Mount would have been familiar not only with the priestly blessing, but also the fact that Torah begins with blessing. When God wants to speak to us, He begins with blessing. Jesus wants to make a clear statement to the crowd that the prophetic word spoken by Isaiah,

I am about to do a new thing; now it springs forth, do you not perceive it? [17]

was about to become a reality. God was indeed doing something new. A number of times Jesus uses the words,

"You heard it said, ..., but I say to you....."

And what better way for Jesus to start His ministry than to start at exactly the same point Father God had done at the beginning; God wants to bless you! Jesus addresses the crowd to give them the new covenant commentary on the old teaching they knew so well. And the commentary was that God had blessed their father Adam in the beginning and now He wanted to bless them with His divine favour and grace. Jesus is going to tell them how to receive it!

-o-o-o-o-

What does blessing mean?

Blessing is to confer or invoke divine favour. The root of the word is to do with being happy and fortunate.

Happy are the people whose God is the Lord [18].

18

The idea behind this statement is that they are really fortunate, even lucky, to have a God like the Lord. Perhaps like me you have been told sometime in your life, "You're lucky to have a faith like yours!" No, says the psalmist, I'm lucky to have a God like mine! Of course I know in Christian parlance we are more likely to use the word *blessed* rather than *lucky* because the former removes the implication of chance or fortune or coincidence. In the New Testament the Greek word for blessed is '*makarios*' and the Amplified Bible describes it as spiritually prosperous, happy, and to be admired. This is why William Young, in his literal translation of the Bible, translates the word *blessed* as *happy*. We could say to each other, *Congratulations! You are under the anointing of the Holy Spirit. I envy you because you have been made so happy by God!*

And Jesus so wants His listeners to obtain this favour that He spells out exactly what they need to do. This was the new thing, a commentary on Torah, the teaching; not to take it away but to make it clear. True happiness comes from looking at life from God's perspective, often the reverse of the usual human point of view, and His intention is that the same blessing is yours today, the same encouragement, the same conditions, and the same results.

-o-o-o-o-

Humbling and Exalting

Before we look at the Beatitudes I want you to understand the very basic principle upon which they are based. God loves the humble and will exalt them. And the reverse is also true. Look at these different verses and you can see how clearly God wants to make the point.

19

All who exalt themselves will be humbled, and all who humble themselves will be exalted[19]

God opposes the proud but gives grace to the humble[20]

Humble yourselves before the Lord and He will exalt you[21]
Humble yourselves therefore under the mighty hand of God, so that He may exalt you in due time[22]

Let the same mind be in you that was in Christ Jesus, who. . . . humbled himself[23]

The Beatitudes are a series of cause and effect statements covering different situations showing us that each time we deny ourselves, humble ourselves before God, or tell Him that we cannot do without Him, He runs to bless us, lift us up and exalts us. If you think you can do it all by yourself, you don't need any help and you already have enough blessing, then the Beatitudes are not for you, but if that is not you, read on!

A Prayer

Father, thank you that you want to bless me, indeed that it is your first thought towards me. Thank you for your word to instruct and encourage me and to show me what you desire. Help me to embrace it that I might live a life to the praise of your glory. Amen

Chapter 4

Blessed are the poor in spirit ...

What is the beginning of this spiritual journey? What does it mean to be poor and especially poor in spirit? I think we will agree that the definition of being poor is to be unable, or have great difficulty, providing for our own needs; to be poor in spirit is the recognition that we do not have the resources to meet our own needs and that we need to turn to Father God for His help.

This is clearly the starting point because it is the very essence of Christianity. That is, understanding that we were made by Father God and that the whole purpose of our being is to enter into relationship with Him and rely on Him and not ourselves for life. The relationship which Adam and Eve enjoyed in the beginning with Father God, of meeting him daily, of walking and talking with Him, was what Father God always intended for us. However, this came to a shattering end when they decided to become self-sufficient and to meet their own needs. "Why do you need God? You can be like him and meet your own needs," was the very deception put before them.

This is obviously the 'norm' for most people today especially in the Western world where spirituality is severely marginalised. It is not difficult to make a good case for not needing God when nearly everything is provided. According to the annual survey of one thousand funeral organisers, the most popular song used at funerals in 2018 was, 'I did it my way'. The sad irony is that while huge numbers of people have taken pride in the fact that they did it their way, I wonder if the reality is that for the vast majority it didn't get them very far and they lived their lives as very pale shadows of what might have been had they walked with God. As Thoreau famously said: "The mass of men lead lives of quiet desperation"[24] and I presume that if he was saying this now he would include the women!

So the very first lesson is to recognise that we are poor in spirit and we need God. Rev. John Notman put it this way. *Being poor in spirit is the opposite of being rich in pride, it is recognising that we are not God, that we need God's help, that we are powerless to change our position and to deal with our unhealthy habits.*[25]

So give up your self-sufficiency. This is the first stage in humbling ourselves.

Self-sufficiency is based in pride and the belief that we have the ability and resources to meet our own needs. This is a very dangerous place to be because it is illusory; there is bound to come a time when circumstances arise that are beyond our control and for which we do not have the necessary resources; probably sooner than later. Maybe we have already experienced this. We get by as best we can but in the vast majority of cases it leaves the scars behind.

But to recognise that we do not have the resources to meet our needs; physical, emotional and spiritual, is the beginning of the journey. It is a position that is the very opposite of proud: humble. We need to admit that Father God can do a better job of running our lives than we can. It is the point at which we declare that we will no longer be self-sufficient but that we will rely on Father God; that we will abandon ourselves to Him, have our sins forgiven, and find that the abundant life that was promised by Jesus is a possibility for us too. Look at what the Bible has to say about these things.

> *It is better to be of a lowly spirit among the poor than to divide the spoil with the proud*[26].

> *The reward for humility and fear of the LORD is riches and honour and life*[27].

23

He has told you, O mortal, what is good; and what does the LORD require of you but to do justice, and to love kindness, and to walk humbly with your God?[28]

But it is by no means certain that we see our position clearly. The letter to the church in Laodicea should make us painfully aware of this. They said,

"I am rich, I have prospered, and I need nothing." You do not realize that you are wretched, pitiable, poor, blind, and naked[29].

Or even worse, the letter to the church in Sardis says,

You have a name for being alive, but you are [spiritually] dead![30]

Oh dear! How could they get it so wrong? How could they be so unaware of the reality of their situation? These are clearly cautionary tales that adjure us rightly to assess ourselves and not be lured into a false sense of security. Equally, it follows that we should not be surprised that making a realistic judgement, and humbling ourselves, will inevitably receive Father God's blessing. But let us also be clear, this is not an insurance policy or some sort of spiritual voucher to be cashed in when there is a problem, and then to go back to the old 'my way' type of life; rather it is a decision, albeit in its infancy, that we will live our lives knowing that we are poor in spirit and that we will hand over our lives to God's control, daily, weekly, monthly, as best we can, and so receive His blessing.

... for theirs is the Kingdom of Heaven

We saw at the beginning that the first statement made by Jesus was,

Repent, for the kingdom of heaven has come near[31]

and Matthew, in his gospel, continually refers to this theme. We have also learned that the Kingdom is with us, here and now. If this were not so the only interpretation of the reward for being poor in spirit would be an eternal one which we would have to wait for until we died, and it also creates a difficulty in explaining the last Beatitude that has the same promise, but more of that later.

Having seen this, what is the blessing for those who acknowledge their need, and humbly ask God for help? I believe it opens a door into the Kingdom of God and the Kingdom becomes *visible,* not with human eyes, but with the eyes of faith that begin to see the unseen. Paul says,

> *We look not at what can be seen but at what cannot be seen; for what can be seen is temporary, but what cannot be seen is eternal.*[32]

Putting it another way, we have acknowledged that we are spiritually impoverished, subject to the rule and reign of God in our lives, and we have therefore become a part of the Kingdom. The apostle John says that we are given power to become the sons of God[33] and as sons we necessarily become citizens of God's kingdom. The benefits of the kingdom are now set before us. Supernatural life is available to us. Jesus tells us to,

> *Seek first His kingdom and His righteousness, and all these things will be given to you as well.*[34]

IF we are prepared to give up our self-sufficiency for God's all-sufficient love, grace and ability, a whole new world will open up for us; the benefits of the Kingdom of Heaven will be ours to appropriate.

A Prayer

Father, when I peel away the layers of pride I so easily portray to other people, and take away the masks I so readily hide behind; when I take a good long hard look at my life, I have to confess there is little there of any substance, and my hold on you is tenuous at best. I confess that my spirit is very poor. The inflow from you is small and the outflow to others is almost non-existent because I'm desperate to keep what little life I have for myself.

I acknowledge that often I am like the people of Laodicea, poor, wretched and blind, and I have a deep poverty of spirit. I bring my brokenness to you and I ask that you will help me to give up my self-sufficiency, which I know does not work, in order that I might discover the riches of life in your kingdom that you have provided through your Son, Jesus Christ, and His sacrifice on the cross of Calvary, and I will receive power to become your child, and find that you are capable of meeting all my needs.
Amen

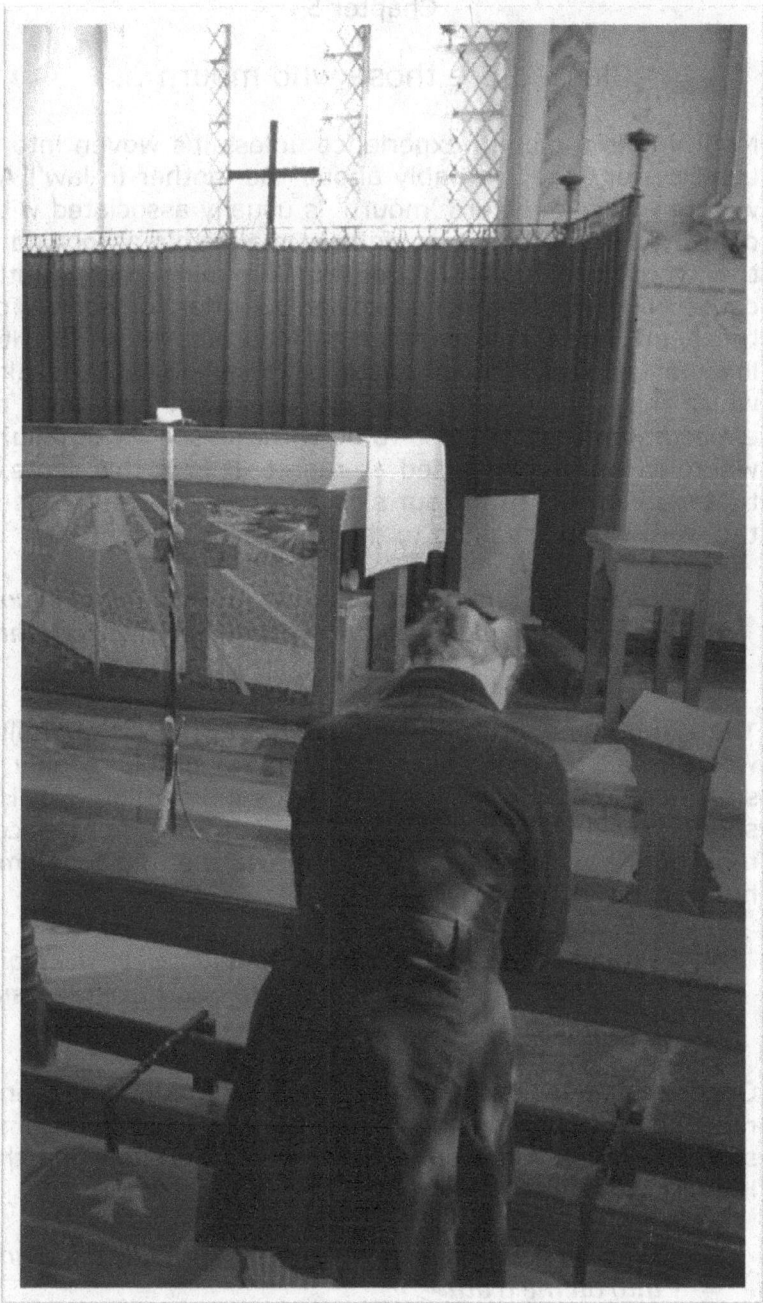

Chapter 5

Blessed are those who mourn ...

Mourning is a painful experience unless it's woven into a Les Dawson joke, probably about 'the mother-in-law'! As we are aware the word 'mourn' is usually associated with death, and although it is right to make this association, the word is actually to do with anything that rightly causes sorrow. It can be defined as grief, or sorrow of the heart, expressed with tears. Mourning is to do with loss: of a loved one, a relationship, a job, a keepsake which has emotional value to us, even the loss of expectation. But it is also to do with the sorrow of failure where it can be expressed as regret. It is in this context that we can mourn for our sins, so the apostle Paul uses the word when speaking to the Corinthians.

> *Is sexual immorality among you? And are you proud! Shouldn't you rather have gone into mourning?[35]*

The Corinthians' attitude was not right. Their immorality was viewed by them as not that big a problem, only a small sin! Paul is filled with righteous indignation. No! He shouts; wail and cry out to the Lord in repentance, mourn for your sin. Paul was also aware of the problems himself. He exclaims,

> *Wretched man that I am! Who will rescue me from this body of death? Thanks be to God through Jesus Christ our Lord![36]*

Once we have become part of God's Kingdom, and recognise we are poor in spirit, humble ourselves, and start becoming more spiritually aware, we soon find the Holy Spirit begins His important work in us.

> *When the Spirit of truth comes, He will guide you into all the truth.[37]*

28

We are suddenly much more aware of our shortcomings. Things that we hardly noticed before, actions, omissions, thoughts, are suddenly thrust into the forefront of our minds, and a creeping conviction that Father God would prefer it if these were not part of our lives, slowly dawns on us. We begin to see ourselves as we truly are and it can be a dark and depressing discovery. Imagine what was going on in Isaiah's mind when he shouted,

> *'Woe is me! I am lost, for I am a man of unclean lips, and I live among a people of unclean lips; yet my eyes have seen the King, the LORD of hosts!*[38]

-o-o-o-o-

At this point, I want to mention two important things in passing. The first is that it is the Holy Spirit's job to convict us, not the job of some well-meaning Christian friend. That is not to say that pointing things out is wrong in itself, but that this is an area so fraught with danger that Jesus directly addressed the issue shortly after the Beatitudes when he asked,

> *Why do you see the speck in your neighbour's eye, but do not notice the log in your own eye? Or how can you say to your neighbour, "Let me take the speck out of your eye," while the log is in your own eye?*[39]

Jesus made it clear that you must,

> *First take the log out of your own eye, and then you will see clearly to take the speck out of your neighbour's eye.*[40]

I remember Juan Carlos Ortiz telling a lovely story about a young woman who shall I say, lived a rather interesting life. She became a Christian and started attending the same church. The church elders were naturally concerned

29

about her lifestyle but were wise enough not to confront her directly about the numerous things they considered needed to be put right in her life. They were spiritual enough to know that this was the Lord's work, but nevertheless thought it might be good if they pointed out the problems to 'the Lord in prayer'. Week by week they prayed for her, asking God to convict her of this, that, and the other. Each week she would come to church and at the appropriate time would confess her sin before the congregation with great earnestness. The problem was that she never confessed what the elders had prayed about! Her confession was always about something that they thought was much too trivial. Week by week the elders sought the Lord again, prayed for the girl, and all but told the Lord that He had made a mistake and overlooked what really needed to be done. This carried on several weeks until the Lord had had enough and told the elders fairly clearly that their agenda was not His agenda, and that He was quite capable of dealing with all the issues in this girl's life in His own good time, and in the order that He thought best. It was an important lesson for the elders to learn, and fortunately without any damage to the young woman, but imagine what might have happened if the elders had actually verbalised their issues directly to her.

And this leads to the second point. The work of the Holy Spirit is to convict not to condemn, but my experience over many years is that there are very few people with sufficient maturity to be able to raise issues without it becoming condemnatory. To be convicted of something is to become convinced of its truth. The Holy Spirit speaks truth to us, causes us to become aware of Father's desire for us, perhaps opens up the possible consequences of our failure to change, and we become convinced that His way is the best way. This is life-giving and up-building. On the other hand, condemnation is an expression of disapproval, a pronouncement of failure, often with the additional threat of, *change or else*, thrown in for good measure. I want to say as clearly as I can that while the Holy Spirit is at work in our lives, God NEVER condemns us. He draws us to Himself by love so that we can proclaim,

> *we love [Him] because He first loved us*[41]

and in view of His mercy, we present to Him our,

> *bodies as a living sacrifice, holy, acceptable to God,*[42]

which is our true and proper worship. We choose not to be conformed to the pattern of this world, but to be

> *transformed by the renewing of your minds.*[43]

-o-o-o-o-

So as the Holy Spirit does His work, we become convicted (not condemned) and begin to realise we are not in such good shape as we thought. Our self-confidence, our laid-back attitude and general feeling of 'I'm OK', and especially, 'I'm no worse than the next person,' takes a direct hit and we begin to mourn for the state we are in.

Let me say this gently. Give up your self-confidence; it will find you out.

The Bible is full of stories about people who were confident everything would turn out alright. Jeremiah tells us,

> *Prophets and priests alike, all practice deceit. They dress the wound of my people as though it were not serious. 'Peace, peace,' they say, when there is no peace.*[44]

In fact disaster was round the corner and just a few years after Jeremiah delivered these words, Judah was taken into captivity in Babylon. As a specific example

31

check out Jeremiah 28 that tells the story of the false prophet Hananiah who prophesied a lie and lost his life for it.

In the lyrics of the musical 'The Sound of Music', we find Maria trying to drum up confidence in herself for what lies ahead, ending up with the conclusion that she has confidence in confidence alone, and finally declaring, without any conviction whatsoever, *I have confidence in me!* I have a better idea. Put your confidence in your heavenly Father who says,

> *Therefore do not worry, saying, "What will we eat?" or "What will we drink?" or "What will we wear?" For it is the Gentiles who strive for all these things; and indeed your heavenly Father knows that you need all these things. But strive first for the kingdom of God and His righteousness, and all these things will be given to you as well.*[45]

Ask the Lord to help you to put your confidence in Him. By all means ask God your questions: How long do I have to wait for you? When will I be free from this or that problem, sin or otherwise? When will I be free from my guilt about my sin? Will I ever be free from the consequences of the sins of others? The questions are real and should not be side-lined. We should never pretend the questions don't exist, but they should not be allowed to deceive us into putting our confidence back into our own hands.

And then there is mourning for other things:
- Mourning for the loss of relationship
- Mourning for the atrocities across the world
- Mourning for the thousands who no longer have a place to call home
- Mourning for ongoing injustice almost everywhere

We mourn and are sorrowful because we empathise with others who are hurting. We also mourn because we have to face up to our total powerlessness. We come to the point where we have no confidence in ME and therefore the blessing is released.

... for they will be comforted

But for those who mourn, those who give up their self-confidence, comfort is on the way! It is the work of the Holy Spirit to convict but also to comfort! The great prophetic passage recorded in Isaiah 61 states,

> *The Spirit of the Lord GOD is upon Me, because the LORD has anointed Me....to comfort all who mourn, to provide for those who mourn in Zion—to give them a garland instead of ashes, the oil of gladness instead of mourning, the mantle of praise instead of a faint spirit.*[46]

In the New Testament, Paul starts his second letter to the Corinthians by praising,

> *the God and Father of our Lord Jesus Christ, the Father of compassion and the God of all comfort, who comforts us in all our troubles.*[47]

In Isaiah 32: 9-20, Isaiah prophesies to the women of Jerusalem. He challenges their complacency and tells them that in just over a year the harvest will fail and their feelings of security will be replaced by trembling with fear. He tells them to respond now with trembling and to put on sackcloth and see things as they really are; that the land is overgrown with thorns and briers. He tells them to beat their breasts and mourn because the fortress is going to be abandoned, the city deserted and the citadel and watchtower will become a wasteland. Until... the Spirit is poured out from on high. Then the desert will become like a fertile field, and the field will seem like a forest. Righteousness will lead to peace, quietness and confidence for ever.

33

This is an amazing passage because the ideas of complacency, mourning, and the coming of the Spirit bringing peace and security, are all dealt with together. This is what God wants to bring to each one of us. Comfort comes from pouring out our hearts to Father about anything that causes us sorrow, internal or external, putting our confidence in Him, and telling Him that without Him we can do nothing, and we are relying on Him entirely. Self-confidence brings anguish, highlights our powerlessness, and develops into an inability to see things as they really are. But confidence in God brings peace and security and the opportunity to

comfort those in any trouble with the comfort we ourselves receive from God.[48]

Praise God!

A Prayer

Father, I am sorrowful about many things. I confess that so often I convince myself that I can do something about them and so often I am wrong. I mourn for my inability to have control over my thoughts and often my actions. With Paul, I cry out to you in anguish, I am a wretched person, who can rescue me? Thank you, thank you, that Jesus can! My desire is to give up my self-confidence, to stop trying and to trust you. Father if you were able to raise Jesus from the dead by your mighty Spirit, I can trust you to do what is needed in my life and I put all my confidence in you because I know you are a Father who loves me and wants the best for me. Help me to receive the comfort of your Holy Spirit and to always be ready to comfort those who I find in similar circumstances. Amen

34

Chapter 6

Blessed are the meek ...

We have acknowledged our poverty and have begun to mourn for our wretched condition, but God is at work in us by His Holy Spirit and His fruit is beginning to grow and develop within us. The next challenge is to produce some fruit!

The fruit of the Spirit is . . . *meekness*.[49] Meek people are those who are dead to themselves, dead to self even though they are still physically alive. This must be clearly distinguished from being spiritually dead the way the church in Sardis was described and referred to in Revelation chapter 3. Spiritual death is to be cut off from the life of God. This 'meekness' death is about becoming non-reactive and only reacting in the way God, by His Spirit, leads us.

Let us look at Jesus for further explanation. Jesus was meek, but we must be very clear that this is not weak. We must remember that it was Jesus, who said,

nevertheless not as I will but as you will.[50]

There was nothing weak about this. Jesus suffered terrible physical abuse, and then suffered a death that is widely recognised as being the cruellest form of execution. He was clearly strong and resolute, and faced a situation that most of us would find too painful even to contemplate. Nevertheless, Jesus was still meek. So Isaiah describes the situation,

> *He [Jesus] was oppressed, and He was afflicted, yet He did not open his mouth; like a lamb that is led to the slaughter, and like a sheep that before its shearers is silent, so He did not open his mouth.*[51]

The word meek has no really sensible English translation, therefore it is variously translated as gentle, mild, or humble, of which the latter is probably the best sense. For instance, Moses is described as

> *very humble, more so than anyone else on the face of the earth.*[52]

In some translations the word 'meek' is used. But what it does describe is not someone who is grovelling, or overly humble on the outside like Uriah Heep from Dickens' David Copperfield, but rather a quiet inner attitude that expresses itself in controlled strength. Jesus described Himself as

> *gentle and humble in heart.*[53]

If we take Jesus as our example, we see that His meekness meant that He laid down His life, died, and trusted Father God to raise Him up by the power of the Holy Spirit to a new resurrection life, and it takes a special sort of strength to be meek in this way. For us it is a conscious decision to lay down our lives, to give them up in order that this meek life of Jesus can be released within us.

So I'm looking for dead people! Perhaps that's a bit strong. Paul says it like this to the Philippians,

> *Let the same mind be in you that was in Christ Jesus, who, though He was in the form of God, did not regard equality with God as something to be exploited, but emptied Himself, taking the form of a slave, being born in human likeness. And being found in human form, He humbled himself and became obedient to the point of death—even death on a cross.*[54]

How do you rate? Let's see!

37

How reactive are you? Do you react to other drivers? Do you react to your husband/wife/partner/friends when they speak sharply to you? What about when someone forgets your birthday or fails to ring you back? Exactly what is it that 'gets your goat'? Just how huffy can you get? As my mentor John Bedford said, "If anyone gets your goat, the only thing it proves is that you had a goat to get!"

The amazing thing is that dead people never react! They are not bothered about ME, they are not self-centred. The world does not revolve around them. They are dead. So Paul takes the argument all the way,

> *I have been crucified with Christ and it is no longer I who live, but it is Christ who lives in me.*[55]

> *Do you not know that all of us who have been baptized into Christ Jesus were baptized into His death? Therefore we have been buried with Him by baptism into death.*[56]

Baptism is a powerful and dramatic physical statement evidencing the spiritual decision to die with Christ. It is a one-time outward expression of an ongoing process. Baptism has a number of parallels in the Bible. We read that the children of Israel were baptised into Moses in the Red Sea, and there is a similar picture as the children of Israel crossed the river Jordan into the Promised Land. All these pictures have two parts to them, first a descent into the water as an act of death, and metaphorically to be buried under it, and an ascent out the water which is a metaphorical resurrection into a new life on the other side. We have entered into death with Christ, been buried with Him, and now we are resurrected into a new life in the Spirit. As Christians, in the words of David Wilkerson, "We do not live the crucified life – we live the resurrected life."[57] Crucifixion was a one-time event, resurrection is a lifestyle! It is no longer my life but His life within me.

38

> *So if anyone is in Christ, there is a new creation:*
> *everything old has passed away; see, everything*
> *has become new![58]*

You have died to your old self. Therefore, give up your self-centredness. We must do it daily, moment by moment, in order that our old lives can continue to die and the life of Jesus continue to grow within us. As Jesus said to the disciples,

> *If any want to become my followers, let them deny*
> *themselves and take up their cross daily and follow*
> *me. For those who want to save their life will lose it,*
> *and those who lose their life for my sake will save*
> *it.[59]*

Die, die, die! This attitude of meekness is towards God first. It is saying to Him that we will accept His will for us as Jesus did and then we will be able to say, what can man do to me, I am already dead. Our attitude to others will also begin to change as we become less reactive to situations as they arise because dead people don't react. We will be able to say with Paul,

> *I have learned to be content with whatever I have.[60]*

We are not controlled by circumstances, because we are not controlled by or occupied with self. This is a continual Biblical theme. Paul says to the Colossians that,

> *as God's chosen ones, holy and beloved, clothe*
> *yourselves with .... meekness,[61]*

and to Timothy he says, as a man of God he should

> *follow after .... meekness[62]*

and to Titus he should show,

meekness unto all.[63]

And to the meek, for those of us who are prepared to lay down our lives, a blessing is released.

... for they will inherit the earth

They will inherit! Now we all know that an inheritance is what someone leaves you when they die. It is impossible for anyone to inherit anything unless someone has died. The question is who has died? I think there are two answers to this. First, Jesus died, and without that happening no one inherits anything, because it is the inheritance from Him that is promised. All of our inheritance comes from and through Him. But His sacrifice and death simply made the inheritance available. For us to take hold of the inheritance we also have to die. That is what this Beatitude is teaching, and Peter makes this perfectly clear in his first letter.

> *Blessed be the God and Father of our Lord Jesus Christ. By His great mercy He has given us a new birth into a living hope through the resurrection of Jesus Christ from the dead, and into an inheritance that is imperishable, undefiled, and unfading, kept in heaven for you.*[64]

He refers to our new birth, which implies a spiritual death, the death and resurrection of Jesus, and our inheritance. If we give up our preoccupation with ourselves, ALL these things will be ours as well. We will become heirs of all that God has to give. The difficulty is that despite the crisis of baptism, the on-going process means that our dying is incremental; we die in part, bit-by-bit, and this means the inheritance is received in proportion to the amount we die.

The inheritance is the Earth. The Old Testament says the meek and the righteous and those the Lord exalts will inherit the land and that is a blessing from the Lord[65] but

40

what does it mean for us, now? This is a difficult question and one upon which the commentators have differing views, if they are prepared to offer any at all. I believe any reference to inheritance must agree with all scripture and we are told that our inheritance is

> incorruptible and undefiled, does not fade away, and is, reserved in heaven for you.[66]

This does not leave me with the impression that it relates to any current piece of real estate! This means that when Jesus spoke, He was referring to two different things. First it is clear that for Israel this was, and has always been, regarded as a reference to the actual land promised to Abraham, Isaac and Jacob. This is what David wrote his songs about and what the Jewish listeners would have automatically understood from Jesus' words as He spoke to them. Jesus offers no further explanation that might have cast doubt in the minds of His hearers as to His meaning. However for us, unless there is a further explanation, the promise becomes meaningless.

We must therefore go back to God's original plan revealed in Adam, that we would walk day-by-day, face-to-face with our God, in the place He had created for us; a plan God still intends to fulfil and has sent His precious Son, our Saviour Jesus Christ to pay the price of redemption. This heaven and this earth will pass away and there will be a new heaven and a new earth[67] and our inheritance is to possess it again and walk and talk with Him and delight in His presence, and Peter encourages us that

> in accordance with His promise, we wait for new heavens and a new earth, where righteousness is at home.[68]

We are heirs of the blessings of the glorious Kingdom of God.

A Prayer

Father I thank you that my inheritance was planned from the beginning; that you said to your people of old that the meek and those you bless would inherit the land. Father I pray that the eyes of my heart may be enlightened in order that I may know the hope to which you have called me, the riches of your glorious inheritance in the saints, and I give thanks to you Father who has qualified me to share in the inheritance of the saints in your kingdom of light.[69] [70] [71]

Father, help me to die daily, to take up my cross and follow you. I give you my self-centredness and acknowledge that everything revolves around you, not me; that it is in you I live and move and have my being.[72]

Amen

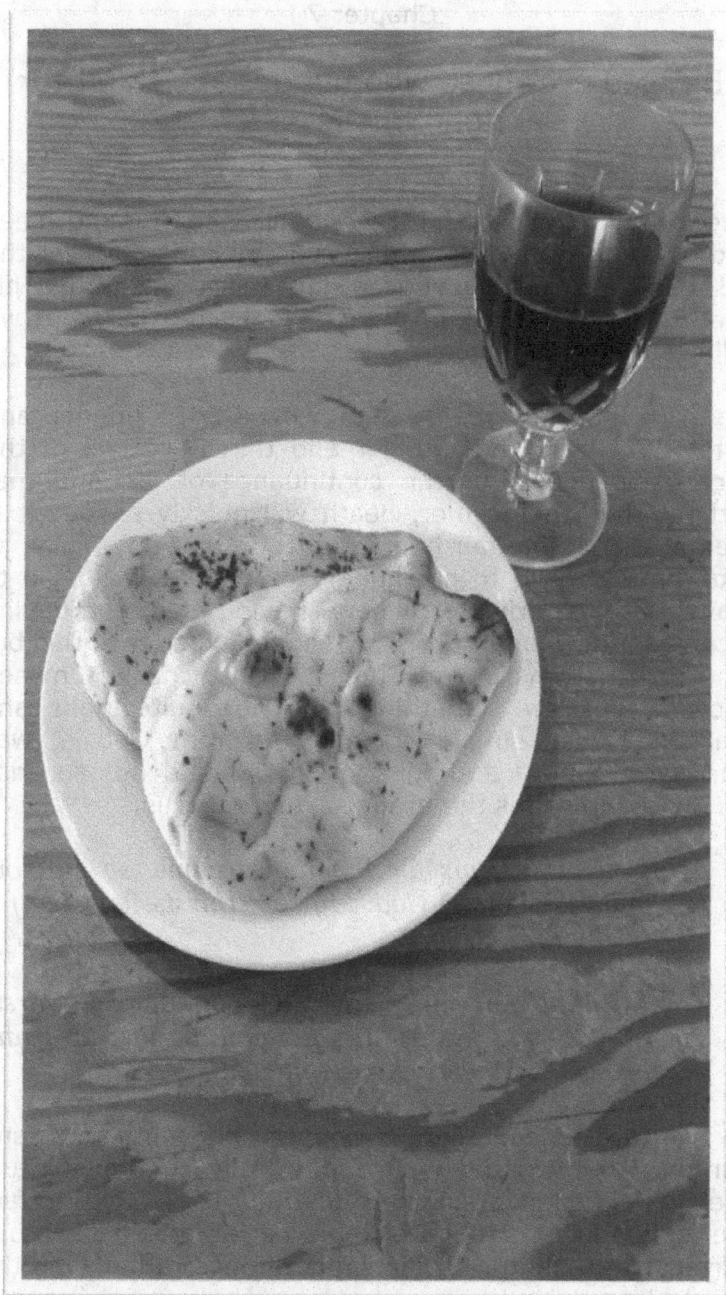

Chapter 7

Blessed are those who hunger and thirst for righteousness ...

Once I have grasped the true significance of being meek and of dying to myself, what I most need is life! Not the old one but a new one, a life based in God. This Beatitude promises it in a slightly obscure way but we will see that life will come.

First, we need to realise that we have to hunger and thirst. We know that hunger and thirst are two of the very basic needs for the continuance of life and that without them being met, death will quickly ensue. It is therefore built into our human function that physically, as soon as we begin to get hungry or thirsty, we begin to crave food and drink. Now here, having died, and having received a new life in Christ, we again experience this but at a spiritual level. Many times I have checked myself because I knew something was not quite right and realised I was simply craving life from God. I was spiritually hungry and thirsty. This should not surprise us. Twice in Psalms the psalmist refers to this.

> *As a deer longs for flowing streams, so my soul longs for you, O God. My soul thirsts for God, for the living God.*[73]

> *O God, you are my God, I seek you, my soul thirsts for you; my flesh faints for you, as in a dry and weary land where there is no water.*[74]

So we are encouraged to apply the hungering and thirsting that we experience physically to the spiritual exercise of building ourselves up in our life in God. In fact the Bible suggests that we would be far better off to use our energy dealing with the spiritual need rather than the physical need.

44

Ho, everyone who thirsts, come to the waters; and you that have no money, come, buy and eat! Come, buy wine and milk without money and without price. Why do you spend your money for that which is not bread, and your labour for that which does not satisfy? Listen carefully to me, and eat what is good, and delight yourselves in rich food. Incline your ear, and come to me; listen, so that you may live.[75]

But it is much stronger than a simple desire. Our physical attitude would be to crave for food and drink on the basis that if we did not get it we would likely die. We need to cultivate the same spiritual attitude. Lord, give me to eat and drink lest I die! Jesus expressed it in a slightly different way by saying that it was the first thing on the agenda.

But strive first for the kingdom of God and His righteousness, and all these things will be given to you as well,[76]

But we know that when it comes to seeking, the hidden attitude that was not mentioned by Jesus is that we should seek with all our heart.[77] So the idea of hungering and thirsting is not one of generalisation or passive interest, but rather one of urgent desire and active seeking.

Secondly, we are told to seek righteousness. I think the simplest way to explain righteousness is that it is whatever conforms to Father's will. Righteousness is an attribute of God and is referred to many times in the Bible. In particular the book of Psalms has so many references to the righteousness of God that they are far too numerous to refer to, but a study of them will be greatly rewarding. In contrast, nearly all the references to righteousness in Proverbs make promises to us if we are righteous. The Righteousness of God in our lives is often simply expressed as being right with God. So the

45

Beatitude is saying that the blessed are those who hunger and thirst, who yearn, for being right with God. This is not any smug morality that has an outer show of innocence, but a deeper, inner desire to be more and more like God Himself.

In other words, we long to be with Father, to be near Him, to go where He goes, to hear His voice even when He speaks quietly, and to receive His life. Father wants us to be like Him; He wants us to long for the same things, He longs for intimacy between Himself and His creation that was His plan from the very beginning. Adam was created for intimacy with God. He was God's son[78] and we have become His sons through Jesus; to those who believed He gave power to become the sons of God.[79] And like Adam, His intention for us is intimacy. But even this fails to appreciate the main point!

When Jesus talks about hungering and thirsting, and eating and drinking, it is a reference to Him. All through the Bible this is true and the concept was there from the beginning. In the Garden of Eden, Adam and Eve were told that they could eat of the fruit of the Tree of Life. The tree was life-giving and a type of Christ. In the wilderness, the children of Israel ate manna, the supernatural bread from Heaven, and they drank the supernatural water from the rock. But the manna and the water were types of Christ. Corinthians spells it out;

The rock was Christ.[80]

Jesus tells the woman at the well that,

Everyone who drinks of this water will be thirsty again, but those who drink of the water that I will give them will never be thirsty. The water that I will give will become in them a spring of water gushing up to eternal life.[81]

Later, Jesus tells the crowd that He is the bread of life.[82] In this amazing discourse, the crowd assert that their forefathers had eaten manna in the desert, but Jesus tells them that it was not Moses who provided the manna but Father God who gives the true bread from Heaven, and that the true bread of God is He who comes down from Heaven and gives life to the world. When the crowd began to grumble, Jesus responds very clearly,

> *I am the living bread that came down from heaven.*
> *Whoever eats of this bread will live for ever.*[83]

The Bible says that this created a significant reaction in the crowd and they argued sharply with one another because the crowd lacked understanding. But for us, surely this is not difficult to understand. Jesus is continually referred to as the person that brings life. This is virtually the subtitle of John's Gospel that right at the beginning declares,

> *In Him was life.*[84]

We were always meant to feast on HIM. Hungering and thirsting after righteousness is ultimately nothing more than hungering and thirsting after God Himself, Father, Son, and Holy Spirit. Jesus goes even further at the last supper.

> *While they were eating, Jesus took a loaf of bread,*
> *and after blessing it He broke it, gave it to the*
> *disciples, and said, 'Take, eat; this is my body.'*
> *Then He took a cup, and after giving thanks He*
> *gave it to them, saying, 'Drink from it, all of you;*
> *for this is my blood of the covenant, which is*
> *poured out for many for the forgiveness of sins.*[85]

Jesus says clearly that what He gave them was His Body and His Blood. This could not have been His physical body and blood because that was sitting beside the disciples at the table, but neither was it simply a representation, commemoration or memorial, none of which do any justice to the words Jesus had previously said,

> *Very truly, I tell you, unless you eat the flesh of the Son of Man and drink His blood, you have no life in you. Those who eat my flesh and drink my blood have eternal life, and I will raise them up on the last day; for my flesh is true food and my blood is true drink. Those who eat my flesh and drink my blood abide in me, and I in them. Just as the living Father sent me, and I live because of the Father, so whoever eats me will live because of me. This is the bread that came down from heaven, not like that which your ancestors ate, and they died. But the one who eats this bread will live for ever.*[86]

When Jesus said this there was an immediate reaction. His own disciples said,

> *This teaching is difficult; who can accept it?*

And we are told that from that time,

> *Many of His disciples turned back and no longer went about with Him.*[87]

This is still a hard saying, but if the two opposing views are not acceptable, there must be a middle view that explains what Jesus meant. In a way that we find difficult to understand, Jesus is spiritually present in the elements during Holy Communion and thereby really feeds us and satisfies our thirst. I believe we can consciously feed on Him, exchanging our corrupt flesh for His life-giving provision.

So we conclude that we cannot provide life for ourselves; we will not try. We will give up self-fulfilment. We will come to an understanding that without His presence our

48

lives will be severely limited and we will hunger and thirst for the living bread that came from heaven.

... for they will be filled

The promise is always that if we ask, we shall receive. How can God refuse to give good gifts to those who ask? When we hunger and thirst for His Son, how can Father refuse? The outcome is inevitable; we will be filled. Hunger and thirst after righteousness and you will receive the living bread and the living water, and be constantly filled.

But here is an interesting spiritual principle. There is a place where we are satisfied but not actually full. Our hunger and thirst has been met, but we are not full. Let's consider these two stories from Elisha.

First there is the story of the widow's oil in 2 Kings 4. Elisha instructs the widow to go around and ask all her neighbours for empty jars, adding, *and not just a few.*[88] I love that! It's clear what's coming. Whatever she brings back is going to get filled, whether it is few or many and so it was.

> *When the vessels were full, she said to her son, 'Bring me another vessel.' But he said to her, 'There are no more.' Then the oil stopped flowing.*[89]

There's the principle, the oil will keep flowing until YOU stop it.

In 2 Kings 13 the story is about Elisha's meeting with King Jehoash, where Elisha is encouraging the King to take spiritual authority over his enemies, the Arameans, by taking his arrows in his hand and striking the ground with them. Elisha instructs the King to do this but does not say how many times which is left for the King to choose. The King strikes the ground three times and stops. The Bible says that Elisha was angry with him and says,

> *You should have struck five or six times; then you would have struck down Aram until you had made an end of it, but now you will strike down Aram only three times.*[90]

Our human reaction is to have some sympathy for the King because how was he to know, but actually it was an exercise in how badly he wanted it. He was satisfied with mediocrity, with his glass being half full. Jesus put it like this,

> *Give and it will be given to you. A good measure, pressed down, shaken together, running over, will be put into your lap; for the measure you give will be the measure you get back.*[91]

When it comes to hunger and thirsting, we will be filled to the measure of our desire. Desire more! Seek more! Reach out for more!

A Prayer

Father, like King David the psalmist, I crave your life; I yearn for your holiness. Sometimes it is as though I am in a desert place and my longing for you is so great, it feels as if I will die unless I can be close to you again. Father I want to give up my self-fulfilment, that I know does not work, and feed on you alone. Thank you for your Son, Jesus, who is the bread and water of life to me. Help me to know you more in the breaking of bread and feed on you in my heart. Thank you for the provision of life, overflowing life. Help me to remember that your ability is limited only by my capacity and desire. May I be filled daily with all the fullness of God.
Amen

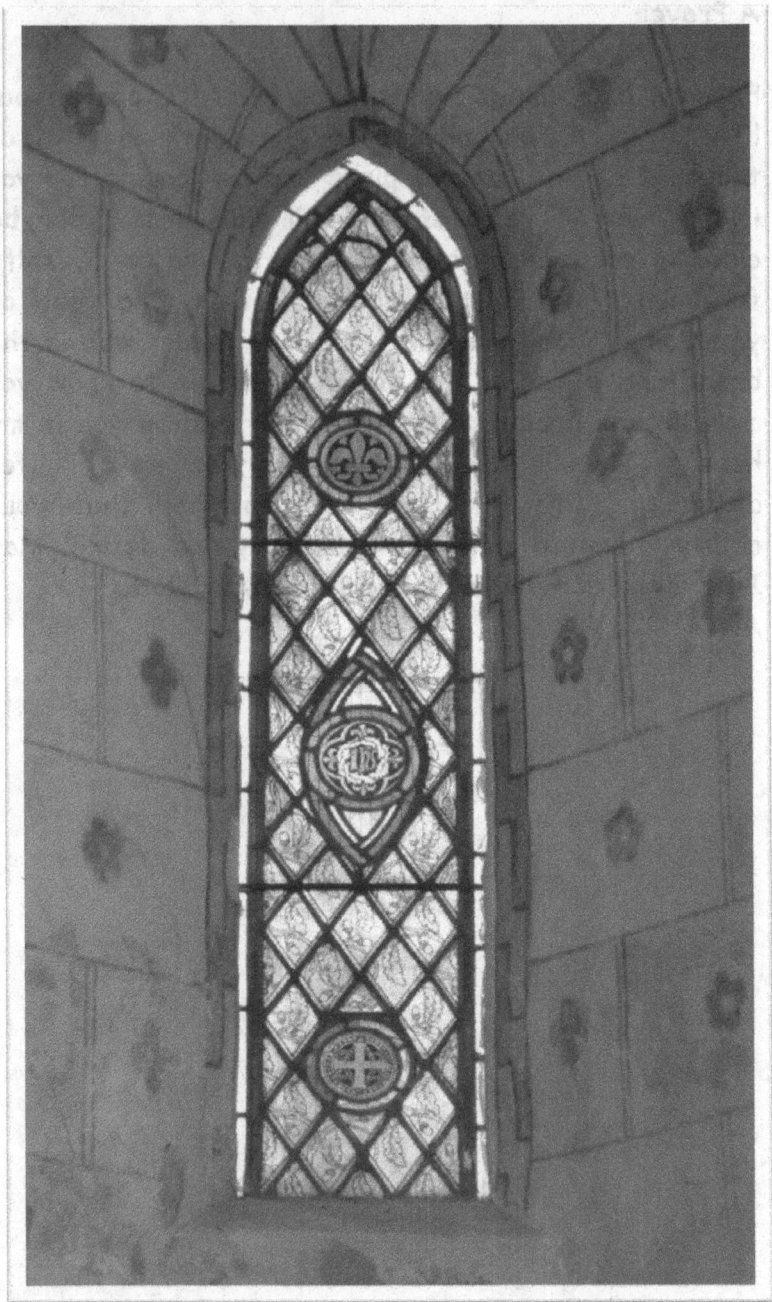

Chapter 8

Blessed are the merciful ...

There is a significant change in the Beatitudes at this point. The first four have all looked at us and been dealing with our own internal state and attitudes, but the focus now changes to the way we relate to others.

We have realised that without God we are nothing; that it is only in Him that we

live and move and have our being[92]

and that our whole bodies, minds and spirits cry out for His presence. We have experienced the ecstasy of His response filling us with His life as the Holy Spirit is released in full measure within us. Now, suddenly we see the world in a different way. I am no different from you. In the words of the old hymn, 'I'm only a sinner saved by grace'[93] and I need God just as much as you.

This attitude blows away the pharisaic position: I'm glad I am not like her! She's a real sinner! Do you know what I've heard about the Pastor? Etc.

You see, the Pharisees thought they were better, that they were not like the ordinary sinners, and that such things could never happen to them. Really? Jesus said,

Let anyone among you who is without sin be the first to throw a stone at her,[94]

and they all disappeared one by one.

Experience is a great antidote to this. Everyone seems to be an expert until they have actual experience of situations - divorce, depression, drugs, or bereavement. There is a smug morality about those who have not actually been through these difficulties and experienced them for themselves; often the only people who really know what they are about are those who have been through them. It is so easy to be right! It is easy to win arguments. It is easy to justify our position. But the question really should be do we want to win the argument or win our brother or sister?

So what is mercy? Mercy is letting someone 'off-the-hook'; it is the opposite of wrath and judgement which is legalistic and harsh; it is not treating a person as they deserve to be treated. Wanting the other person to 'get what they deserve' is an emotion I am familiar with and one that I find pops up at regular intervals. Perhaps that is your experience too. Even Jesus referred to it,

> *You have heard that it was said, An eye for an eye and a tooth for a tooth[95],*

But He is saying there is a better way, and we have seen in Chapter 5 that we have to be very careful about judgement. Mercy is about treating others, when they make mistakes, in the way we ourselves want to be treated when we make mistakes. I want Father God **and you** to treat me mercifully; not to punish me as I deserve. James tells us that,

> *Mercy triumphs over judgement[96]*

Mercy means knowing where we have come from; the understanding that we do not have it all together and that we daily need the life of the Father filling us. It is about love, so give up your self-righteousness.

In 1 Corinthians 8, Paul is confronted with a problem about eating meat sacrificed to idols. Some of the people in the church in Corinth considered such meat to be defiled spiritually and therefore not to be eaten. Paul says they think this because

> *Their conscience is weak,[97]*

54

He argues that there is but one God, the others being no more than *so-called gods*[98], and that,

> *No idol in the world really exists.*[99]

It follows therefore that the meat offered to something that does not exist cannot be defiled. So, does he start preaching about freedom and maturity in Christ, telling them they need to grow up, shape up and understand their freedom in Christ in deeper measure? Of course not! On the contrary, what he says is to tell the more mature to,

> *Take care that this liberty of yours does not somehow become a stumbling-block to the weak.*[100]

In fact Paul goes further by saying to them that if they exercise their freedom without concern,

> *By your knowledge those weak believers for whom Christ died are destroyed. When you thus sin against members of your family, and wound their conscience when it is weak, you sin against Christ.*[101]

This turns the situation right on its head. Rather than castigating the weakness of the immature, he issues a severe warning to the more mature that they should be very careful lest they are the ones found in sin. Paul ends by saying that if what he eats causes his brother to fall, he will never eat meat again! He will ensure he does nothing to make his brother fall. He would rather love than be right. One of the sayings of my great friend and mentor, John Bedford, was, "It is better to be loving than right!" I call it the law of love.

Paul makes it clear that what is needed is love. We will be merciful to our brothers and sisters because we have been this way before. We used to be immature; we used to be weak; we once needed to be loved in this way and still bear the scars of the tongue-lashing of our elder brothers. Therefore we will be merciful and loving. And this amazingly also applies to sin.

> *If anyone is detected in a transgression, you who have received the Spirit should restore such a one in a spirit of gentleness.*[102]

This is in the present continuous tense meaning it is an on-going process and it is clear it should be done in love and humility; in case you find yourself in the same position you should,

> *take care that you yourselves are not tempted.*[103]

And for those who will embrace this, give up their self-righteousness and be merciful, there is a blessing - a congratulations!

... for they will be shown mercy

Do you ever think that with God there are some strange anomalies? I find it difficult that a God who pours out His grace upon us, who lavishes His love upon us knowing there is an inexhaustible supply,

> *who forgives all your iniquity, who heals all your diseases, who redeems your life from the Pit, who crowns you with steadfast love and mercy, who satisfies you with good as long as you live, so that your youth is renewed like the eagle's,* and who is, *merciful and gracious, slow to anger, and abounding in steadfast love* and **who does not deal with us according to our sins, nor repay us according to our iniquities,**[104]

can then make His mercy and forgiveness conditional! And yet this is a continual message to us.

56

And forgive us our sins, as we have forgiven those who sin against us,[105]

for judgement will be without mercy to anyone who has shown no mercy.[106]

Give and it will be given, show mercy and you will receive mercy. This is how it works in the Kingdom of God. God gives a little and we give it away, so God gives us more, and we give that away, so we receive even more. Do you remember the words of Jesus, quoted twice in Matthew:

For to those who have, more will be given, and they will have an abundance; but from those who have nothing, even what they have will be taken away.[107]

This is God's principle of life.

Do not judge, and you will not be judged; do not condemn, and you will not be condemned. Forgive, and you will be forgiven; give, and it will be given to you. A good measure, pressed down, shaken together, running over, will be put into your lap; for the measure you give will be the measure you get back.[108]

If you want more, give away what you have! His life, love, forgiveness and mercy are meant to be shared. It is more blessed to give than to receive.[109]

A Prayer

O all-embracing mercy, Thou ever open door, what should I do without thee when heart and eyes run o'er?
When all things seem against me, to drive me to despair, I know one gate is open, one ear will hear my prayer.[110]

Father, freely you have given to me and you ask me now to freely give. That is my desire. I admit that you have not treated me as I deserved; that you have treated me with abundant mercy and grace. Please help me to treat others in exactly the same way, not to repay evil for evil but to repay evil with good. Please remind me that I am only what I am today because of your love, and remind me from where I have come. Please help me to make this the basis for how I see and treat others. Help me to be merciful to others in the way you have been merciful to me.
Amen

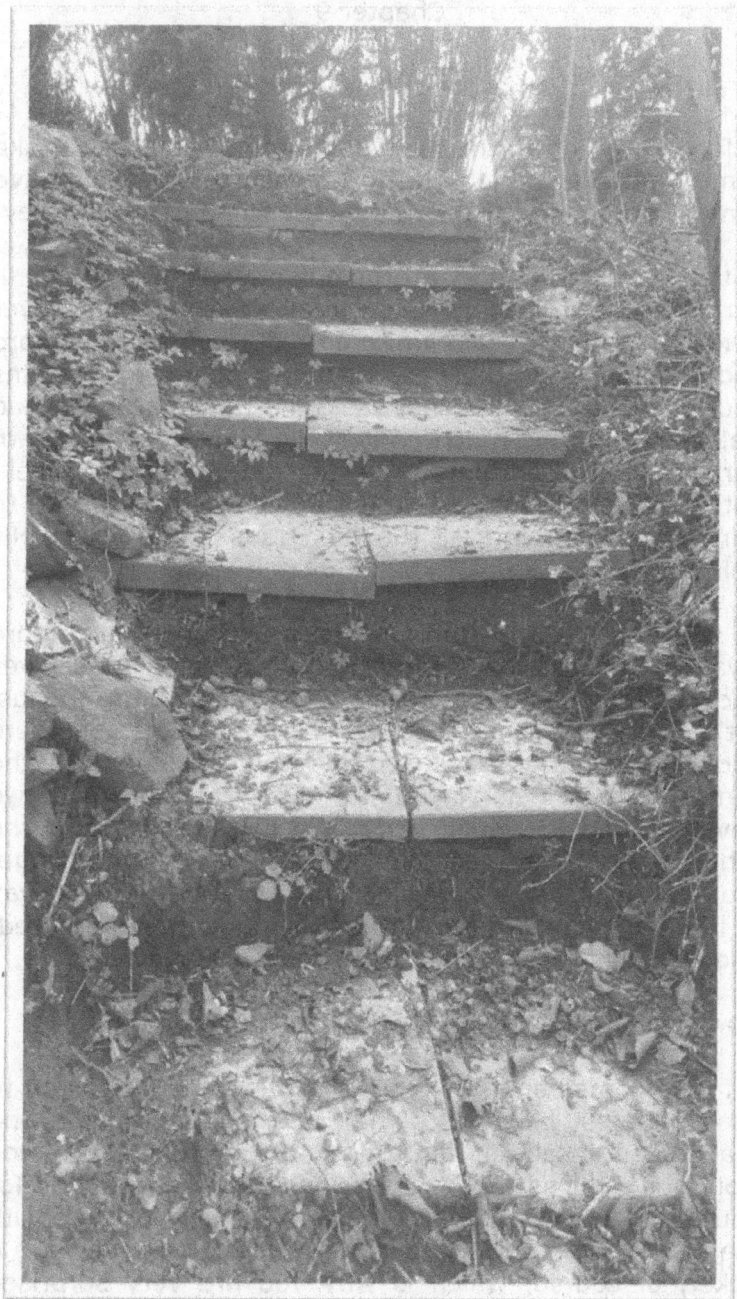

Chapter 9

Time Out

Before we go on to the next Beatitude, I want us to take some time out and look back to consider where we have come from and the point we have reached in our journey.

Initially, we became aware of our poverty of spirit, and perhaps some readers even realised they had never made an initial firm commitment to Jesus as their Lord and Saviour. From there we began to mourn for our sins and for our loss of life that we could have had if we had walked with Jesus much earlier. We learned to lay down our lives and start putting Jesus first, becoming meek, not weak, and at last got to the point where we began to hunger and thirst after the life Jesus gives us by His Spirit.

As we began to walk in the spirit, we became much more aware of the growth of the fruits of the spirit in our lives and began to treat people as God treats them and us, with mercy, realising that we are no better than them and, but for the grace of God, we would be in exactly the same position. I think you will agree that the place we have reached is a good place. We can look back on the progress we have made and actually see some change. We have made significant inroads into the 'my way' way of life and the self-sufficient, self-confident, self-centred, and self-fulfilling attitudes we once held so dear.

Now I would like you to consider this modern parable.

A friend comes and tells you that they have just been to see the latest blockbuster film at the local cinema and that it was absolutely amazing and they really think you would enjoy it as well, and so they are willing to pay for you to go. They hand you an envelope that you take with thanks. What do you expect to see in the envelope? A ticket, of course, which is why you are very surprised when you find that the envelope contains a large number of tickets, one for every showing of the film for the next two weeks, and also a little note that simply says, 'Use all the tickets. Enjoy!'

Now you have a dilemma. You realise your friend has been extremely generous in providing all these tickets, but there is now a significant expectation on you; your friend had a financial cost but you are now expected to repay that cost with your time. Nevertheless, you want to see the film and you have nothing to lose, so you take the first ticket and go. The film was all your friend reported and was very enjoyable, so you decide to use the second ticket. To your amazement, on seeing the film the second time you noticed a considerable amount that you hadn't noticed the first time and that whets your appetite, so you decide to use the third ticket and again notice various things you had missed in previous visits. You use a number of tickets until you know virtually the whole script word perfect, you know the nuances in the changes of voice, you have picked up one or two small errors in the continuity, and eventually you come out having seen the film yet again and the only new thing you have noticed is a sly look in the background between two of the main characters.

You now consider the position you are in. You have received very little benefit from the last ticket you used despite the fact that the cost of every ticket, from the first to the last, was the same both in terms of money and time. There are still a few tickets left. You finally decide that you will not use them (or give them away!) because what you perceive you will gain does not justify the cost of your time, notwithstanding that your friend has paid the price for them.

This is obviously an extreme scenario but one that we face day by day in small ways. It is also a picture of the Christian life. When the majority of people become Christians, they do so 'on a ticket' of having their sins forgiven and the hope of eternal life. It takes a little while

61

to realise that it is not a single ticket that has been given, but a book of tickets where there are several for each day of our lives. The tickets are grouped in various ways: church, prayer, purity and holiness, outreach, Bible reading, etc. Some tickets cost us very little, church on Sunday, a quick prayer here and there, occasionally something requiring a little more commitment like reading through the Bible in a year, and each one of us decides which tickets we will use. It is this process, whereby we have to work out our salvation; that He must increase and we must decrease; that we have been given power to become the sons of God - it is clearly not a one-off event, but an ongoing process.

I have taken this time out, and included this parable and explanation, because in the journey through the Beatitudes, I believe this is where many Christians decide to stop. They get to this point and the perceived cost of going on is greater than the perceived benefit.

Why is this? There are basically two reasons. The first is that we can become satisfied with where we have reached on the journey. We look around and see that we are already ahead of many Christians (though we know we should never compare like this!), we know how to hunger and thirst after righteousness and be filled, and have allowed this to be outworked in ministry to others in love, pastoral care, perhaps even healing. Without necessarily feeling boastful, or particularly proud, as we have agreed above, we do think we have reached a good place; and it is a good place and we have done well to reach it, **but there is more**.

The second reason is that we can take a look at the next Beatitude, and our perception is that 'purity of heart' is going to cost rather more than we have paid in the past, and in addition to that, the perceived benefit is small and quite vague. What does it really mean to see God? No one thinks that this means physically, at least in this life, and in the absence of any further explanation, there seems very little to be gained and a great cost to pay.

As a result, I believe many followers of Jesus settle for five out of eight. And in any event we still have the final ticket in our book, eternal life!

So there is a big decision to make. Are we prepared to trust Father enough to pay the price and see what He will do? I confess that it has taken me a good part of my life to push past this point; but Father has more for us. I want to encourage you to go on, take another step, but before you make up your mind, let's see exactly what this next Beatitude is about.

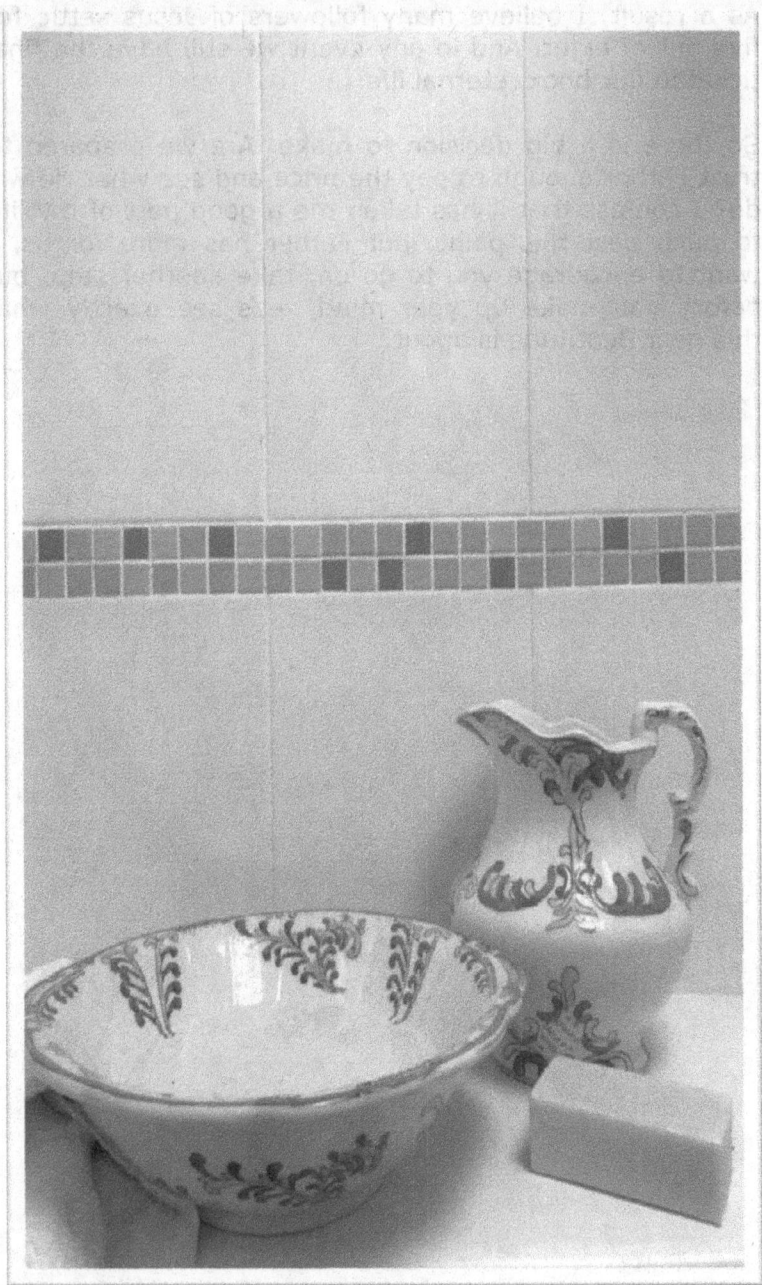

Chapter 10

Blessed are the pure in heart ...

We have had a little move out from ourselves and been entrusted with taking God's mercy and love to others, but before extending this, there is something within us that needs dealing with. Before we can make much further progress we will have to deal with our purity of heart.

We all know that our heart is the physical part of us that pumps the blood around our bodies, but it has also come metaphorically to mean our total intellectual and moral life; our personality, emotions and feelings, thought processes, and decision-making, and when the Bible refers to 'the heart', this is what it means; the complete non-physical make-up of me as a person. Now the Bible has some not very good things to say about our heart. Jeremiah tells us that,

> The heart is deceitful above all things, and desperately wicked[111]

and worse still, Jesus confirms it in no uncertain terms:

> for out of the heart come evil intentions, murder, adultery, fornication, theft, false witness, slander. These are what defile a person.[112]

Wow! Something needs to be done with my heart. God says it needs to be pure. What is your understanding of being pure? Is it like the three wise monkeys: see no evil, hear no evil, speak no evil? Or is it even think no evil! And then who decides what is evil anyway? Is it God, or your favourite preacher's interpretation of scripture, or a voice from the past, a parent or teacher?

Actually, purity is about the degree of mixture, the internal make up of a substance. The less mixture there is, the more pure the substance. Spiritually, it is to do with cleansing and refining on the inside. Purity of heart is about having no mixture, not being double-minded, which literally means two-souled. As mentioned in the previous chapter, purity of heart is not something to be taken lightly or easily achieved. When gold or silver is refined, or made purer, the process is to heat it up until it melts, and this allows the impurities to come to the surface where they are skimmed off. The metal is then allowed to cool and the process is repeated, getting more pure each time until the required purity is reached.

The very thought of this process being applied to me makes me shudder! Salvation is free, but working it out is costly. And yet I desperately need it. There seem to be a lot of things mixed in there, not very pure. I also want at this point quickly to deal with the difference between purity and holiness that are often confused. Purity is a measure of the substance itself, whereas holiness is primarily about separation and what an object is used for. Holiness is to be set aside and used for only one purpose. The following diagram might be helpful.

	Impure	Pure
Unholy	Made of anything and used for everything	Made of pure substance but used for everything
Holy	Made of anything but only used for one purpose	Made of pure substance and only used for one purpose

So the vessels used in the temple were pure and holy, that is, they were made from pure gold and they were only ever used for worship in the temple, and the application for us is that our purity is a measure of our

66

internal spirituality, and our holiness is a measure of the balance of devotion to Father God and other things. Now we understand what purity is about, let us see how it is applied. The word is used in the story of the leper who comes to Jesus and asks to be healed. He says,

> *If you choose, you can make me clean.*[113]

In this case he is saying, my body is mixed with disease, it needs to be made pure or clean, and I need to have the disease removed so that my body is no longer a mixture of good and bad. Consider these verses:

> *They worshipped the LORD, but they also served their own gods.*[114]

> *No slave can serve two masters; for a slave will either hate the one and love the other, or be devoted to the one and despise the other. You cannot serve God and wealth.*[115]

> *You cannot drink the cup of the Lord and the cup of demons. You cannot partake of the table of the Lord and the table of demons.*[116]

> *With [the tongue] we bless the Lord and Father, and with it we curse those who are made in the likeness of God. From the same mouth come blessing and cursing.*[117]

In all these verses we see there is mixture. James continues,

> *Does a spring pour forth from the same opening both fresh and brackish water? Can a fig tree, my brothers and sisters, yield olives, or a grapevine figs. No more can salt water yield fresh,*[118]

> *Cleanse your hands, you sinners and purify your hearts, you double-minded.*[119]

67

All these illustrations merely confirm the sad situation that these issues do affect all of us. We are affected because we believe that Father God is not able, or is unwilling, to meet our need of love and acceptance, so we take matters into our own hands and seek it elsewhere. James' conclusion is,

My brothers and sisters, this ought not to be so,[120]

and Father God is saying, get rid of the mixture! So all that is now required is for us to give up our self-gratification! King David asks the question,

Who shall ascend the hill of the Lord? And who shall stand in His holy place? Those who have clean hands and pure hearts.[121]

John reminds us,

See what love the Father has given us, that we should be called children of God; and that is what we are. Beloved, we are God's children now; what we will be has not yet been revealed. What we do know is this: when He is revealed, we will be like Him, for we will see Him as he is.[122]

But the very next verse says,

And all who have this hope in Him purify themselves, just as He is pure.[123]

David tells us that we need to be pure in order to come close to God. James instructs us to be pure on the basis that mixture creates nonsense, with blessing and cursing coming from the same mouth, and John appeals to us on the basis of Father's great love. It is Father's great desire to be close to us; He wants to recreate the relationship that He first had with Adam, but with you and me! The price for this to happen has been paid, not with money but with the blood of his precious son Jesus Christ. No wonder it does not come cheaply for us. I have suggested above that many shy away from this step because it is not easy, but like everything with the Christian life, God is looking at our hearts and is not expecting us to have the ability to do it on our own. It is Father God

> who is at work in you, enabling you both to will and to work for His good pleasure.[124]

I believe therefore that desire is the only requirement. If we truly want to deepen our relationship with the Lord, and we want a pure heart, God will begin this process simply if we tell Him so. David, when he was seeking restoration after his adultery with Bathsheba, sought God for a clean heart with an impassioned plea set out in Psalm 51.

> Have mercy on me, O God, according to your steadfast love; according to your abundant mercy blot out my transgressions. Wash me thoroughly from my iniquity, and cleanse me from my sin (vs1-2) Purge me with hyssop, and I shall be clean; wash me, and I shall be whiter than snow .(v7) Create in me a clean heart, O God, and put a new and right spirit within me (v10)

The French hymn writer expressed his heartfelt desire in his great hymn:

> Oh, the bitter shame and sorrow, that a time could ever be, when I let the Saviour's pity plead in vain, and proudly answered,
> All of self, and none of Thee,
>
> Yet He found me; I beheld Him bleeding on the cursed tree; heard Him pray, forgive them, Father, and my wistful heart said faintly,
> Some of self, and some of Thee,

Day by day His tender mercy, healing, helping, full
and free, sweet and strong, and ah! so patient,
brought me lower while I whispered,
Less of self, and more of Thee,

Higher than the highest heavens, deeper than the
deepest sea, Lord, thy love at last hath conquered;
grant me now my heart's petition,
None of self, and all of Thee.[125]

The process is not easy. Father God will treat us as sons
and we know that with son-ship comes discipline.

*My child, do not regard lightly the discipline of the
Lord, or lose heart when you are punished by Him;
for the Lord disciplines those whom He loves and
chastises every child whom He accepts.*[126]

The Bible says that our Heavenly Father uses a number
of means to produce purity within us. Sometimes it
comes through testing as with Job,

*but He knows the way that I take, when He has
tested me, I shall come out like gold,*[127]

sometimes through challenging our faith, as with the
early church,

cleansing their hearts by faith,[128]

and sometimes by requiring obedience,

*now that you have purified yourselves by obeying
the truth.*[129]

But we should be continually aware that this is all
happening because Father God and we have a great
mutual desire to be close in relationship; this is what we
were made for. He paid the price; will you? Will you take
this big step and give up more of yourself than you have

possibly ever done before? Will you trust your heavenly Father and believe

that He rewards those who seek Him.[130]

Will you seek purity, because the outcome is the blessing that we will see Him?

... for they will see God

We have already mentioned that the promise of seeing God is a little vague from a human perspective, and hard to fathom. We know it is not meant to be a physical sight while we are still alive, as the Bible makes it clear that no man or woman can see the Father. Even more, we are told that the Father is spirit and is invisible! It is therefore not surprising that with these words lodged in the back of our memories, we are slow to respond to the idea of seeing God. We content ourselves with the belief that we will see Him in eternity and this must be the explanation; no wonder our motivation is not great.

Reading numerous commentaries, the response to this Beatitude is interesting. Much is made of being pure, but little is said about seeing God. One commentary did not mention this verse at all! But Father clearly meant something by it and I believe that the promise means to be blessed in this life, not just in the life to come. So what can we make of it?

First I want to introduce the concept of glory. The Bible talks at great length about the glory of God; the wonder, the awe, the splendour, the majesty, the greatness of His power and ability; our all-seeing and all-knowing God. It talks about His creation, telling of His glory[131] and that we should,

Ascribe to the LORD the glory of His name.[132]

Wherever God goes there is also a manifestation of His glory. He cannot go without it! So whether it is the tabernacle in the wilderness,[133] or Solomon's temple,[134] the glory of the Lord appears. When people saw God, they saw the glory and were greatly affected by it.

I believe that to see God means to get close enough to Him to be affected by His glory. What does this mean? Isaiah 6 tells us of Isaiah's vision of Heaven where he got close enough to see and hear. He sees the Lord and the angels, he hears the worship, and he hears God speak. It is interesting to note that his immediate response to seeing God was to connect it to and declare his lack of purity. And yet the fact that he was there is testimony that this lack was not sufficient for the experience to be denied him. Therefore, we can deduce that as purity is not absolute but relative, so our ability to come close to Father is proportional. The purer we are, the nearer we get, and the clearer we see and hear.

So let us take this idea further, and understand how 'seeing God' will bless us. Let us consider something simple. To see anything means to be within visual sight. I suggest that seeing God, which we know is not physical, means to be in His presence; within seeing distance in the same way as we would describe as being within earshot. Close enough for us to see what He is doing and hear what He is saying. It is upon this very concept that Jesus tells us He operates. Several times in John's gospel He says that He only does what He sees the Father doing, and only says the words He hears the father saying.[135] Clearly Jesus was not talking about a physical seeing and hearing, but closeness to Father that meant in the Spirit, He got a clear view and unimpaired hearing of what Father wanted. The communication between the Father and Jesus was absolute because Jesus was completely pure.

Although limited, this is what happened to Isaiah, and Exodus tells us about Moses' encounter with God. He saw the back of God and returned from the meeting with a face so reflecting the glory of God that the people could not look at him directly. We can react with amazement at this but what is really amazing is that the Apostle Paul teaches that Moses' encounter does not compare to our own experience! Paul asks,

> *How much more will the ministry of the Spirit come in glory? For if there was glory in the ministry of condemnation, how much more does the ministry of justification abound in glory!*[136]

This is the beginning of glory of which we will hear more. And it is in this context that we find the promise that,

> *all of us, with unveiled faces, seeing the glory of the Lord as though reflected in a mirror, are being transformed into the same image from one degree of glory to another.*[137]

We see that the glory is not something that is inherent in us but it is the glory of the Father that is reflected in us. Sin separates us from the glory of God[138] but if we purify ourselves, we get closer and closer to the Father, and the reflection only grows from glory to glory. To see Him is to reflect His glory.

What an amazing blessing? To see God is to be included at a more and more intimate level with what He is doing in your world, and to have an increasing amount of His glory reflected in you. God's offer is that as we continually work towards purity, becoming more pure as He is pure, so we will get nearer and nearer to Him, and we will see what He is doing and hear that still, small voice in greater and greater measure, and go on from one degree of glory to another.

Will you pay the price?

A Prayer

Refiner's fire, purify my heart, let me be as gold and silver, purify my heart let me be as gold, pure gold.[139] Father I have sung this many times and even when singing these words, I am so doubleminded that I have found myself thinking about something else. Father I do not want to be like this. My heart longs to be near you, I want to see you; I want to live my life close to you, being able to hear the whisper of your heart. Hear my cry and work in me by your Spirit that I may be pure before you and so day by day I may be involved with what you are doing, and I may reflect more and more of your glory to those around me.

Amen

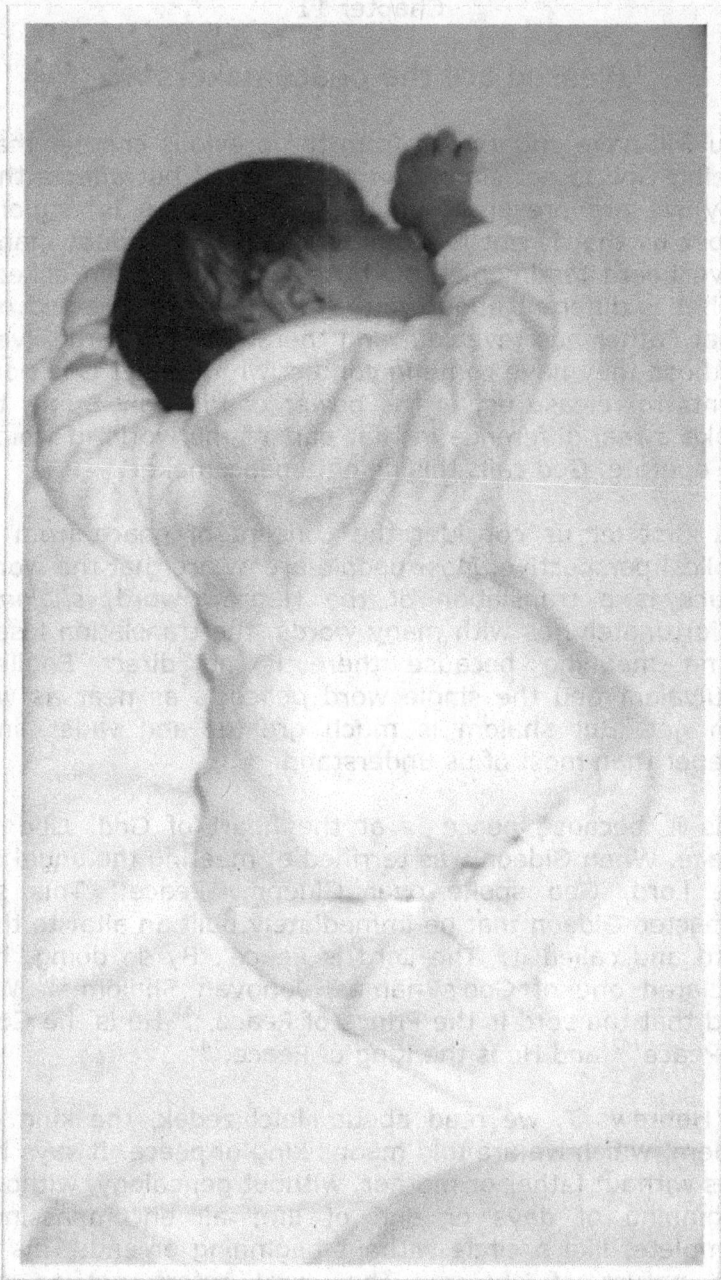

Chapter 11

Blessed are the peacemakers ...

You will have understood from the previous chapter that seeing God is not simply an end in itself but affects the way we are presented to the world. There is a glory about us that is not humanly explained. No doubt many have heard testimonies of those who have been asked, "What is different about you?" And some have acted on what Father has revealed, and thereby touched the lives of those they have come in contact with. Father God now wants to release us, in the power of His Holy Spirit, to make a real difference in that part of the world in which we operate. God calls this being a peacemaker.

But first let us consider the concept of peace from a Biblical perspective. Most people are aware that the word *peace* is a translation of the Hebrew word, *shalom.* Unfortunately, as with many words, the translation loses some meaning because there is no direct English equivalent and the single word *peace* is as near as we can get. But shalom is much greater and wider and deeper than most of us understand.

This is because peace is at the heart of God. God is peace. When Gideon was terrified at meeting the angel of the Lord, God spoke over Gideon, "Peace!" This so impacted Gideon that he immediately built an altar to the Lord and called it, 'The Lord is Peace'. By so doing, he declared one of God's names, Jehovah Shalom.[140] We find that the Lord is the Prince of Peace,[141] He is the God of Peace[142] and He is the King of Peace.[143]

In Hebrews 7, we read about Melchizedek, the king of Salem, which we are told means king of peace. It says he was without father or mother, without genealogy, without beginning of days or end of life; all encompassing, complete, like a circle without beginning or end. This is the nature of shalom. The word refers not to an individual feeling but to a state of affairs, one of peace, contentment, security and confidence. The best single word to describe it is probably not *peace* but *completeness* because it embraces well-being at every level. Strong's Concordance defines it as completeness, wholeness, health, peace, welfare, safety, soundness, tranquillity, prosperity, perfectness, fullness, rest, harmony, the absence of agitation or discord. Wow! Who doesn't want some of that? And Father God wants you and me, and others, to experience and enjoy it. Are you at this sort of peace? It is your birthright in God; part of your inheritance. Let these verses bless you.

Submit to God and be at peace with Him[144]

Righteousness and peace will kiss each other[145]

Those of steadfast mind you keep in peace— in peace because they trust in you.[146]

The effect of righteousness will be peace[147]

The punishment that brought us peace was on Him.[148]

Peace I leave with you, my peace I give to you.[149]

To set the mind on the Spirit is life and peace.[150]

The fruit of the Spirit is.... peace.[151]

We can see that our 'shalom' was purchased for us by Jesus through His suffering; that it was the last gift Jesus conferred on His disciples before He ascended into heaven. It is one of the fruits of the Spirit that is worked in us as part of our sanctification, and it is also a matter of submission and being right with God. Paul puts it at the top of the list in the words,

and let the peace of Christ rule in your hearts[152]

77

where the word *rule* is better translated *beginning,* and therefore Paul is saying let the peace of Christ be the first thing in your life; let it be the beginning of all things. Shalom is the very essence of our life in God. It is therefore an amazing thing that we should be called to be peacemakers, and entrusted with taking this peace to a hurting and lost creation; to go as Father God's representatives to broker peace on His behalf.

But first, can I encourage you to seek this peace for yourself, and address your own lack of peace in any area. We may long to be used by God, we may see the need, we can become desperate to minister God's peace, but we must be aware there is always a danger in ministering God's life where we are not ourselves receiving it. It can lead us into the difficulty of saying '*do as I say'* rather than '*do as I do',* and while the Lord is gracious and merciful to us in the short term, He will not allow it to continue for long. It is much safer, that before we attempt to be peacemakers, we are enjoying a good measure of peace with Father ourselves. So go back and meditate on the verses above on page 77 and let the peace of God really begin to rule in your heart.

Now let us consider the Beatitude itself, and see exactly how Father wants to bless us, and what He requires of us in order for this to happen. Being a peacemaker is to bring two or more warring parties together. In a spiritual sense, this means to bring the people and the Saviour together. The distance between the two varies enormously, and has many different reasons, but both of these are incidental to us as peacemakers. We come alongside in obedience to Father, to what we have seen and heard. Now I want to give you some general examples so you can see how being a peacemaker may apply to you.

1. Salvation
Salvation is the declaration of peace between God and man. It is peace WITH God. Peace with God comes when

you believe by faith, and receive Jesus as Lord and Saviour.

> *Therefore, since we are justified by faith, we have peace with God through our Lord Jesus Christ[153]*

And we have been entrusted with this amazing ministry.

> *So if anyone is in Christ, there is a new creation: everything old has passed away; see, everything has become new! All this is from God, who reconciled us to Himself through Christ, and has* **given us the ministry of reconciliation![154]**

We have been reconciled to God through the cross of Jesus, and it is our privilege to take the same gospel to others so that they too may be reconciled to God, and enjoy peace and relationship with the Father.

2. Anxiety

Anxiety is an uncertainty and worry regarding the future; an absence of peace, but there is a peace OF God which is beyond understanding, and which is based in faith and relationship, and lifts us above circumstances. Problems do not magically disappear, but there can be a peace in them.

> *Do not worry about anything, but in everything by prayer and supplication with thanksgiving let your requests be made known to God. And the peace of God, which surpasses all understanding, will guard your hearts and your minds in Christ Jesus.[155]*

This is what Paul is talking about when he says he has learned the secret of being content whatever the circumstances, whether in need or in plenty.[156] Paul does not allow circumstances to thwart the rule of God's peace in his life and therefore he is always content.

79

It is for us to take this peace to anxious, worried, and hurting people, and to minister it to them; to tell them there is a peace to be experienced even in their trying circumstances; to pray for them and to ask for God's peace in their lives, and maybe even declare it prophetically over them.

3. Health

There is never any shortage of people asking for prayer about their health. All of us get sick from time to time and we are dis-eased. The completeness of shalom has been broken, and it is therefore perfectly legitimate to pray for its restoration. Whether we pray for healing, or health, or wholeness, or peace, really does not matter, and will probably be different in every situation, but we should be ministering peace in this way.

4. Welfare

Jesus told the story of the Good Samaritan with which we are all familiar.[157] The essence of the parable was to challenge the crowd to answer the question: who was the true minister of peace? Was it the religious people who passed by on the other side or was it the foreigner who actually did something? We know it was the one who went and tended the wounds, bound them up, and arranged for ongoing care. Time and again we are encouraged to bear one another's burdens,[158] mourn with those who mourn,[159] and simply love one another.[160] Or then maybe it is simply someone who is hungry, or thirsty, or is a stranger, or who needs clothes, or is in prison, and then when the Lord rewards us, and we wonder why, He says,

> *Truly I tell you, just as you did it to one of the least of these who are members of my family, you did it to me.*[161]

5. Blessing

We learned at the beginning that the first thing God wants to do is to bless His creation. Therefore, speak a

80

blessing, give away peace. Shalom is a blessing, a manifestation of the divine grace, and an impartation of God's life upon, and into, another human being. Why not bless someone? Why not bless someone today?

Of course, being a peacemaker can sometimes not be peaceful; it can be quite stressful and some are called to go where it can even be dangerous. The very nature of peace-making is to be between parties who are in conflict, and at a physical level, stories appear at regular intervals of people who attempt to bring peace in a situation and end up being caught in the cross-fire, whether with fists or knives or worse. We are continually counselled to keep away and clear of such issues. Spiritual peace-making can also get us into trouble. Anyone who has knocked doors knows that the reception varies enormously, but as peacemakers we obey the prompting of the Lord and put ourselves into situations where the Lord can use us.

This can seriously stretch our faith! Father may ask us to do and say things that under normal circumstances we would never consider. Even Jesus had to spit on the ground, make mud, and put it on someone's eyes. Let's be realistic, this probably stretched the norms even for Jesus' time, let alone now. A lady once came to me for prayer for a bad back and the Lord told me to pick her up and shake her. This is not something I was accustomed to do or actually, had ever done before. After a struggle with myself, I obeyed and she was healed; peace reigned in that situation for her and eventually for me!

It is no good being self-conscious. Give it up! We are whole, complete, and our confidence is in Him!

... for they will be called children of God

For those who will minister God's peace, there is a special blessing, and it is interesting because it is not what it seems at first. We are to be called children of

God. Now this is strange because our understanding is that we are already called children of God. We have acknowledged our sin, accepted the gift of God by faith in the Lord Jesus Christ, and His death on our behalf at Calvary; the same Spirit that raised Jesus from the dead has also raised us up and set us free from the law of sin and death, and the seal of the Spirit has been given to us so that we can now cry, Abba!, Father![162] Paul tells the Romans that,

> *for all who are led by the Spirit of God are children of God*[163]

and John exclaims,

> *See what love the Father has given us, that we should be called children of God; and that is what we are.*[164]

We are already His children, and we are already called this irrespective of any ministry of peace. It is therefore clearly not God who calls us 'His children' when we are peacemakers. So who is it that will call us the children of God? It is none other than the people who have received the peace of God from and through us. It is they who will recognise who we are and bear witness to it. *Surely this was a child of God!* People will see our love, and by this shall all men know we are [His] disciples.[165] Even their enemies knew that Peter and John had *been with Jesus.*[166] You see,

> *peacemakers who sow in peace raise a harvest of righteousness.*[167]

The world recognises that these people have been with Jesus and they will say the same about you and me. Seek God for this anointing, earnestly desire it; abandon yourself to Father and go and minister the peace of God to a needy world and they will say about you, "This is a child of God!"

82

A Prayer

Father, I confess there are many parts of my life that are not at peace; that do not have the wholeness, well-being, tranquillity, rest and harmony that you intended for me; the peace that was purchased for me by the blood of Jesus at Calvary. I acknowledge that your peace is my birthright; it is part of my inheritance, and therefore Lord I claim it as a child of yours. Father, I ask that in all those hurt and broken areas of my life you will bring your peace. I give you again those parts of my life where I am still not submitted to you; those parts where there is still unrighteousness, and I ask that you will forgive me and restore me again. Bring the fullness of your peace to my life in the name of Jesus. And I ask that then I would take your peace to a needy world to bring your shalom; to preach the good news of reconciliation to God, to bind up the broken-hearted, to release the prisoners, to comfort all who mourn, to heal the sick, and proclaim the Lord's love to all those to whom you would send me, in the name of Jesus.

Amen

Chapter 12

Blessed are those who are persecuted because of righteousness ...

We have nearly completed our journey. We have denied ourselves, taken up our cross and followed Him. We have walked down the hill of self-effort and slowly up the hill of the Lord, and we are now approaching the pinnacle with the last statement of how we need to position ourselves in order to receive Father's blessing. This Beatitude seems to have been doubled up and I think it is good to reproduce it in full here.

Blessed are those who are persecuted for righteousness' sake, for theirs is the kingdom of heaven.

Blessed are you when people revile you and persecute you and utter all kinds of evil against you falsely on my account. Rejoice and be glad, for your reward is great in heaven, for in the same way they persecuted the prophets who were before you.

When I read this, two well-known responses, perhaps familiar to you, come to mind.

I don't believe it!   You cannot be serious!

Surely if we are to reach the maximum the Lord has to offer, then we should be reading:

Blessed are those who worship in spirit and truth;
Blessed are those who pray without ceasing;
Blessed are those who love their neighbour as themselves;

but surely not blessed are those who are persecuted.

So, in the context of the Beatitudes, what does persecution refer to? Does it mean a feeling of suffering or discomfort?

Every time we deny ourselves, there is an element of suffering in the sense that we are doing something that we would prefer not to do. Take fasting, which the Bible encourages us to practice, and is reasonably widespread even if not regular. It is generally accompanied by some feeling of discomfort that is accepted as a part of the process. The amount of suffering will vary from person to person and may not be that great, but it is there. However, the main point here is that it is internal and we have complete control over the situation, and we can choose if we wish to continue or not.

Persecution has a completely different feel. It is external and comes from a third party over whom we have no control. You can hear this being said by the psalmist when he cries out,

> *They persecute me wrongfully; Help me!*[168]

He is being persecuted; there appears to be no reason for it, but he cannot stop it. They will not listen to reason so he asks the Lord to step in.

Are we surprised by all this; should we be surprised? Definitely not! The Bible makes it absolutely clear that we should expect it because it was promised to us all. Jesus said,

> *If they persecuted me they will also persecute you*[169]

and Paul told Timothy,

> *all who desire to live a godly life in Christ Jesus will suffer persecution.*[170]

It really cannot be clearer than this. These statements are backed up by dozens of different accounts of persecution from the lives of Bible characters. A very rough check will soon take you to the lives of Moses, Job,

Elijah, Micaiah, Hanani, Zachariah, Jeremiah, Daniel, Shadrach, Meshach and Abednego, Peter, John, Paul and Silas, all of whom suffered for their faith, and there were clearly hundreds more about whom Paul generalizes in his letter to the Hebrews, but without any suggestion of minimizing their experiences, by saying they

> *had trial of mockings and scourgings, yes, and of chains and imprisonment. They were stoned, they were sawn in two, were tempted, were slain with the sword. They wandered about in sheepskins and goatskins, being destitute, afflicted, tormented— of whom the world was not worthy. They wandered in deserts and mountains, in dens and caves of the earth.*[171]

It is suffering, over which we have no control, and comes simply because we name the name of Jesus Christ and swear our allegiance to Him. The whole of history bears witness to the truth of persecution. Apart from the Biblical accounts that are there for all of us to consider, Miller's Church History[172] gives chronological details of the early persecution under Nero and Domitian, the martyrdom of the early church fathers, persecution in Asia Minor, France and Africa, and the later persecution under Maximin, Decius, Valerian, and ultimately Diocletian who made a concerted attempt to wipe out the whole of Christendom.

But did this only happen in ancient times? Of course not, there are numerous current stories of persecution, and if you want to read some and pray for Christians being persecuted, I recommend you to read Barnabus Fund reports that can be obtained from their website. And what is God's response to these people? Look at the passage above and see these words, "of whom the world was not worthy." These people, from ancient times and modern times, were too good for this world, and the world did not deserve to have such amazing people in it. That's Father's heart!

Nevertheless, do I want to be persecuted? Not really, it is not something that immediately appeals to me. I do not regard myself as brave in any way and naturally I would shy away from pain of any sort. I am not like one of my relatives who relished the physical confrontation of playing football and rugby, the harder, the better! But will I be persecuted? Possibly, the time may come in the western world, and some think it will be sooner rather than later, when simply being a Christian will create serious opposition. Already the Christian church has been marginalised in the UK, and to give a Christian viewpoint almost always elicits an accusation of bigotry.

Further, I am convinced that if any of us go down the High Street, in any town, and do what Jesus did, persecution will follow very quickly and in exactly the way that Jesus predicted. The issue for the Christian church in the UK, and possibly in the western world, and the challenge of this particular Beatitude, is that the vast majority of Christians are not going down the High Street and doing what Jesus did. Let us consider the position of Moses in ancient Egypt. This is what the Bible says about him.

> *By faith Moses, when he became of age, refused to be called the son of Pharaoh's daughter, choosing rather to suffer affliction with the people of God than to enjoy the passing pleasures of sin.*[173]

The first thing to note is that he made a conscious decision to do something entirely within his own control. He refused to be known as the child of Pharaoh's daughter and by implication the Pharaoh's grandson. Stop and think of the reaction that would follow if Prince Harry suddenly announced that he was joining the Salvation Army and no longer wanted to be regarded as Prince Charles' son or the grandson of the Queen. Now the immensity of Moses' decision becomes apparent. The incredulity, the questioning, the anger was no doubt faced by Moses; and he chose this.

88

Shadrach, Meshach and Abednego, whose story is told in Daniel 3, chose to face death rather than bow to a false god. When they were given a second chance by King Nebuchadnezzar, their response was unequivocal.

> O Nebuchadnezzar, we have no need to answer you in this matter. If that is the case, our God whom we serve is able to deliver us from the burning fiery furnace, and He will deliver us from your hand, O king. But if not, let it be known to you, O king, that we do not serve your gods, nor will we worship the gold image which you have set up.[174]

In other words, we will not defend ourselves before you because we believe our God will deliver us from death, but even if He doesn't, we will still not bow down. What a choice! What courage!

What about Paul, he continually put himself back into danger. This is what he says about himself.

> I have worked much harder, been in prison more frequently, been flogged more severely, and been exposed to death again and again. Five times I received from the Jews the forty lashes minus one. Three times I was beaten with rods, once I was pelted with stones, three times I was shipwrecked, I spent a night and a day in the open sea, I have been constantly on the move. I have been in danger from rivers, in danger from bandits, in danger from my fellow Jews, in danger from Gentiles; in danger in the city, in danger in the country, in danger at sea; and in danger from false believers. I have laboured and toiled and have often gone without sleep; I have known hunger and thirst and have often gone without food; I have been cold and naked.[175]

My immediate reaction to all this is, how long will it take him to learn? Why does he continually go back for more, why does he keep choosing this way? But then I discovered his attitude was very different from mine.

> *When we are cursed, we bless; when we are persecuted, we endure it; when we are slandered, we answer kindly. We have become the scum of the earth, the garbage of the world – right up to this moment.*[176]

> *We are hard pressed on every side, but not crushed; perplexed, but not in despair; persecuted, but not abandoned; struck down, but not destroyed.*[177]

So the cost we are being asked to pay is very clear, and we have seen that before any of us make a decision where cost is involved, we mentally, consciously or unconsciously, weigh up the benefits against that cost. What is the benefit or reward?

... for theirs is the kingdom of heaven
... for great is your reward in heaven

The first of these is interesting because this is exactly where we started the journey. This was the reward for those who were poor in spirit, and we seem to have gone round in a circle, but is it the same? I don't think so. I believe the first of these is an offer of what is in store and what might be, whereas at the end of the journey, it is an attainable reality as we shall see. Otherwise, these two statements, while full of meaning to us, probably meant very little to the original hearers who at that time had little or no concept of the Kingdom, and must have wondered exactly what rewards were on offer. Of course Jesus was very soon to continue His teaching by encouraging His listeners,

> *do not lay up for yourselves treasures on earth, where moth and rust destroy and where thieves break in and steal; but lay up for yourselves treasures in heaven, where neither moth nor rust*

90

destroys and where thieves do not break in and steal.[178]

Later we find some commentary on this as Paul made it clear what their rewards were.

> *You joyfully accepted the plundering of your goods, knowing that you have a better and an enduring possession for yourselves in heaven.*[179]

Now we see this put into practice by those who were persecuted by having their possessions taken from them; that they were joyful in their loss because they were sure of their treasure in heaven that could not be stolen from them.

Earlier we looked at Moses, and his testimony was that

> *he regarded disgrace for the sake of Christ of greater value than the treasures of Egypt because he was looking forward to his reward.*[180]

Wow! Disgrace was more valuable than the inheritance he could have received from being Pharaoh's grandson; but of course it was not the disgrace that was better but the reward he knew he would get that he had already 'banked' by faith. Paul's response was not in the future but in the present.

> *(We) always carry around in our body the death of Jesus so that the life of Jesus may be revealed in our body.*[181]

Paul was prepared to identify, if needs be on a daily basis, so closely with the death of the Lord that part of his life would also experience death, in order that in its place the resurrection life of Jesus would be manifest in him. This was the reward.

Even Jesus went through the same experience when being persecuted and falsely accused and suffering the ultimate penalty of losing His life. It was

> *for the joy set before Him (that He) endured the cross.*[182]

His suffering was accepted because He already knew there was a reward for Him in heaven. I want to let Paul have the last word here because the whole matter is summed up in one verse.

> *Now if we are children (of God), then we are heirs, heirs of God and co-heirs with Christ, if indeed we share in his sufferings, **in order that we may also share in His glory.**[183]*

It's all about GLORY. The reward, the taking hold of the Kingdom is about sharing the glory of the Lord. What indeed could be more glorious? We have seen the beginnings of this earlier when we dealt with purity, but now we see this come to its fruition. Moses suffered the persecution resulting from his decisions, but his reward, even under an old covenant, was to be welcomed up the hill of the Lord, and to see the glory of the Lord so greatly that when he returned to the people they had to shield their eyes.

Stephen suffered false accusation and was arrested and put on trial before the Sanhedrin, where he gave his hearers a history lesson of God's faithfulness to them and their unfaithfulness to Him, sufficient for them to be furious with him, but then,

> *he, being full of the Holy Spirit, gazed into heaven and saw the glory of God, and Jesus standing at the right hand of God and said, "Look! I see the heavens opened and the Son of Man standing at the right hand of God!*[184]

Stephen witnessed to the glory of God and reached out and took hold of it in their very presence. No wonder it was too much for them; those who neither saw nor experienced it. Stephen received his reward.

It is easy to assume that such reward comes at the same time as physical death, but this should not be our focus. Glory was manifest in Stephen even before this time. He is described as,

> *full of faith and power,*

and that he

> *did great wonders and signs among the people.*[185]

It was this, and his ability to contend with false arguments with wisdom and in the power of the Spirit, that created the persecution in the first place. We should see that all persecution is the pathway to glory.

A Prayer

Father I find it difficult to imagine persecution of the sort we read about and yet the Christian press is reporting it today and every day in other parts of the world. I am unable to pray for persecution but I do pray that I would be used by you and that if persecution results from it, that you would prepare me. Help me Lord never to shy away from your purposes in my life through fear of the consequences, and cause me to so follow you that I may eventually become one of those of whom the world was not worthy, and may it all be for your glory.
Amen

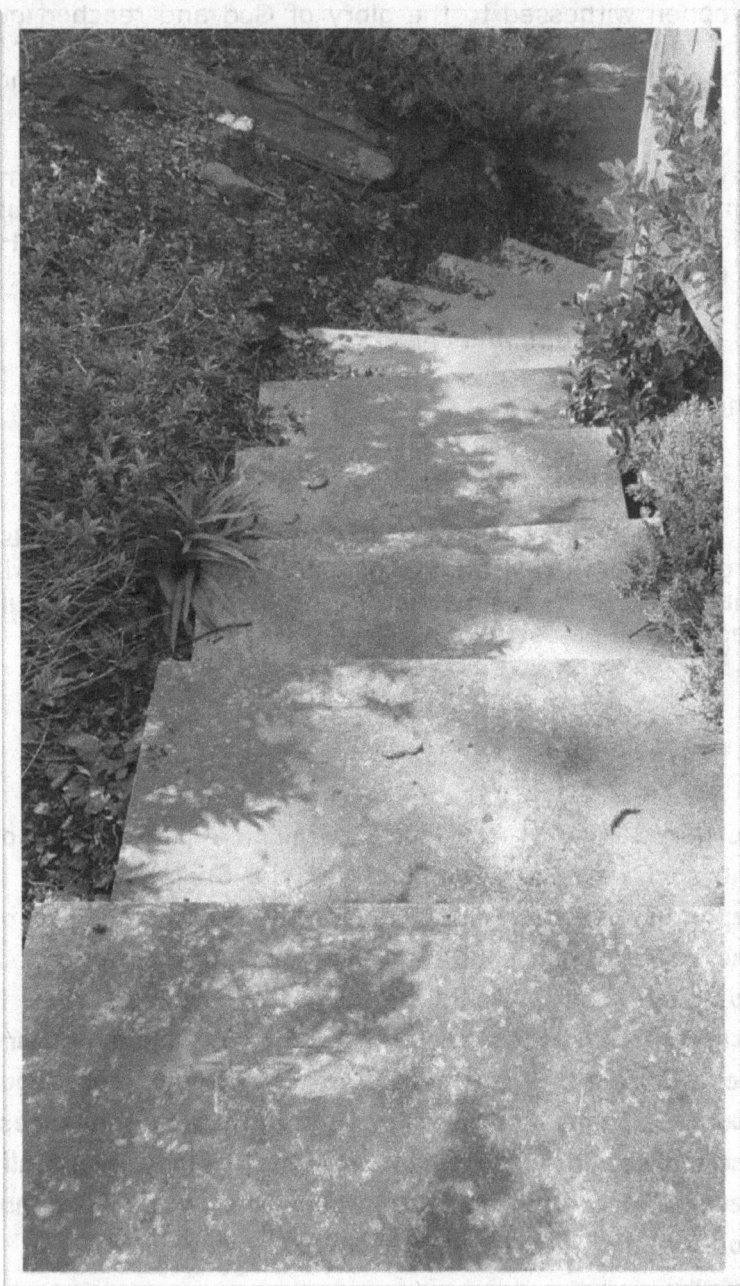

Chapter 13

Take Another Step

I'm going to introduce the concept of building backwards which is very simple but important. For example, the more that is built, the more there is to maintain, and if no maintenance takes place, eventually the new building program and the decay of the previous building reaches equilibrium, and even though new building is taking place, there is no increase, because the old falls down at the same speed as the new is being built. If this idea is changed to a block of flats, it can be seen that simply building new floors, and failing to maintain what has already been built, will eventually cause the whole building to collapse, the new as well as the old.

It is vitally important that in addition to continuing up the hill of the Lord, the past lessons are maintained until they become a way of life, and there is very little deviation from them. It is for this reason that remembrance is such an important Biblical concept. God continually tells us that He remembers[186] and He expects us to do the same.[187] As a result, I want quickly to go back over what we have learned as a remembrance and as a checklist, so we can get the complete picture.

We saw that to be blessed was to receive divine favour, and that the root of the word was to do with being happy and fortunate. In ancient times, everyone had their own God; imagine two people are talking about their lives and one gives testimony to the grace and favour he has received at the hand of God. The other exclaims, 'You are really lucky to have a God like yours; mine is useless and is just a piece of wood at the side of the house and does nothing'. Now we begin to see what being blessed means. This is **what** it is, but the process of being blessed is to give up your life and receive God's life in exchange.

The correct theological word for this is sanctification, but I believe that this word has of recent years taken on a negativity and has become associated with sterile evangelicalism, whereas it should be seen as a vibrant, active, and dynamic life exchange. So the more of your life you give up, the more you invoke God's favour and the more of His life you receive.

The Beatitudes take you through the steps of the journey from the top of your own self-made hill, the Hill of Self, to the glory of resurrection with Him at the top of the hill of the Lord.

King David asked,

> Who shall ascend the hill of the LORD? And who shall stand in His holy place?[188]

And his answer,

> Those who have clean hands and pure hearts, who do not lift up their souls to what is false, and do not swear deceitfully. They will receive blessing from the LORD, and vindication from the God of their salvation. Such is the company of those who seek Him, who seek the face of the God of Jacob.[189]

We have tried to answer the same question from the Beatitudes, albeit in more lengthy terms.

We have found out:

1. The place to start is to acknowledge being poor in spirit; that there is a poverty that may be carefully hidden from the outside view, but that prevents any significant flow of life to and from Father and to and from the people we meet day by day. It is the recognition that we are not self-sufficient.

96

```
        HILL of SELF              HILL of the LORD

   H      Poor                    Persecuted      E

   U                                              X

   M      Mourn                   Peacemaker      A

   B                                              L

   L      Meek                    Pure            T

   E

          Hunger                  Merciful
```

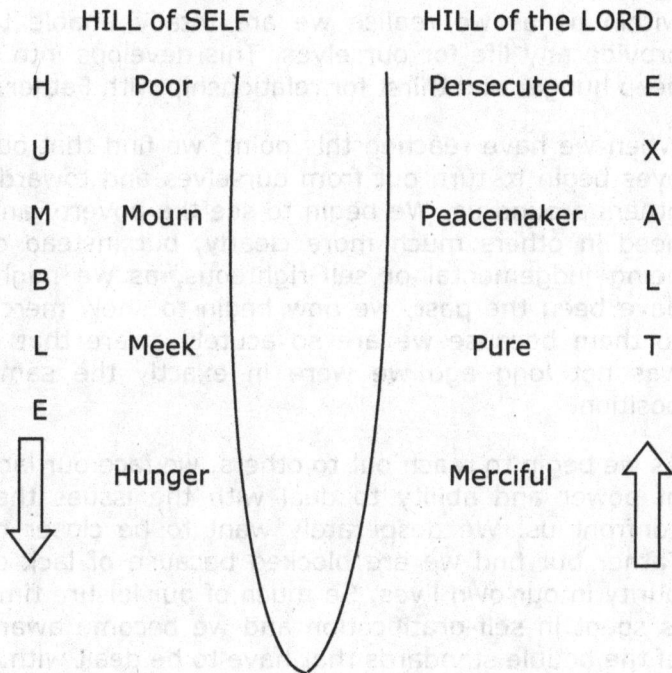

2.   Once we recognise that we are not self-sufficient,
     we begin to mourn our condition and reach out to
     Father God for the flow of life from Him that will
     make a difference in our lives. Our self-confidence
     takes a knock and we slowly begin to put our faith
     in Father.

3.   We then begin to realise how self-centred we are,
     and how we regularly take up the position that the
     whole world revolves around us. We now have to
     face laying down our lives and becoming meek, in
     order that the life of Father God can be manifest in
     us.

4.   As we become less and less self-fulfilling and self-satisfied, we cry out more and more for Father's life within us as we realise we are totally unable to provide any life for ourselves. This develops into a deep hunger and thirst for relationship with Father.

5.   When we have reached this point, we find that our eyes begin to turn out from ourselves and towards others around us. We begin to see the poverty and need in others much more clearly, but instead of being judgemental or self-righteous, as we might have been the past, we now begin to show mercy to them because we are so acutely aware that it was not long ago we were in exactly the same position.

6.   As we begin to reach out to others, we face our lack of power and ability to deal with the issues that confront us. We desperately want to be closer to Father but find we are blocked because of lack of purity in our own lives. So much of our leisure time is spent in self-gratification and we become aware of the double standards that have to be dealt with.

7.   Once we have reached a level of purity that enables us to hear what God is saying, and be aware of what He is doing, we become much clearer channels of God's life into the myriad of situations we find ourselves in day by day. We are no longer self-conscious, but will gladly take and give away Father's life into the events that confront us.

8.   The ultimate outworking of this is that we become more and more like Jesus; our lives are hid with Christ in God; we no longer self-assert our own lives but we become one with Him in his sufferings, and begin to portray His glory in ever increasing measure. Hallelujah!

Next Steps

In closing, I want us to be clear about three things. First, we have received God's life but we did not deserve it, earn it, or achieve it; it is not a 'deal' we can negotiate with God; it is all a gift of grace as we humble ourselves before Him because of His amazing love for us. Our righteousness is still as filthy rags; at best we are still unprofitable or unworthy servants, only having done what our duty demanded, but by giving up our own lives we have allowed God to pour His life into us as a completely mis-matched exchange; new for old, good for evil, life for death.

Secondly, let's not pretend that this is an easy journey; it takes courage and perseverance, and sometimes just sheer commitment. The writer to the Hebrews is trying to encourage us.

> *Therefore, since we are surrounded by so great a cloud of witnesses, let us also lay aside every weight and the sin that clings so closely, and let us run with perseverance the race that is set before us, looking to Jesus the pioneer and perfecter of our faith, who for the sake of the joy that was set before Him endured the cross, disregarding its shame, and has taken His seat at the right hand of the throne of God.[190]*

Did you realise that Jesus walked this path before us? He laid aside all His glory, all His privilege and He humbled Himself and became obedient, and when persecution came, there was a cross at the top of the hill, and still He was obedient. Therefore, glory came! God exalted Him to the highest place, gave Him a name that is above every name, and the day will come when everyone, from the least to the greatest, from the richest to the poorest, those who made the journey and those who did not, will at the sound of His name, bow down before Him and acknowledge that Jesus Christ is Lord.

Thirdly, although I have presented this study as linear, life is not actually linear in that way. None of us simply keep on getting better (or worse), at best we take two steps forward and one back, so it is better to understand life as a series of circles, where we often backtrack or go over ground we have already covered. I do not suppose there is a single reader that does not identify with this. But the important thing is not to be worried about the times we regress as long as the general movement is in the direction of the Lord's leading. If we falter or fall, we look up, we get up and go again; if we sin, we repent and go again. Or sometimes, when we feel we have moved on significantly in our life, made real progress, another area pops up and we have to start all over again. I do not suppose there is a single reader that does not identify with this. When it happens, go back to Chapter 4 and start over, applying the principles to the new issues the Lord has uncovered. He is making you more like Himself. Hallelujah!

Check the questions on page 6 again. Did you write down your answers at the beginning, and can you answer differently now?

-o-o-o-o-

I have learned that I am still nothing without Him; I can achieve nothing of eternal significance without Him. He has become my life. I am still on the journey; I have still not arrived, but I am still ascending the hill of the Lord. Can I encourage you, even urge you, to take another step to do the same?

The Lord will bless you and keep you; the Lord will make his face to shine upon you and be gracious to you; the Lord will lift up the light of his countenance upon you and will give you His peace.

I praise you Lord Jesus Christ, you have the words of eternal life; I praise you Lord Jesus Christ, King of endless glory.
Amen.

Notes

AV   Authorised Version
NIVUK New International Version - UK
NKJV   New King James Version
NLT   New Living Translation

Chapter 1
[1] Matt 6.11
[2] Matt 4.4
[3] John 6.35
[4] Acts 17.28
[5] 1 Sam 26.23
[6] Heb 11.6

Chapter 3
[7] Matt 4.17
[8] Matt 4.23
[9] Luke 17.20-21 NKJV
[10] Luke 10.11
[11] Matt 5.2-12
[12] Gen 1.22
[13] Gen 1.28
[14] Num 6.24-26
[15] Num 6.27
[16] Mark 10.16
[17] Isa 43.19
[18] Ps 144.15
[19] Matt 23.12
[20] James 4.6
[21] James 4.10
[22] 1 Pet 5.6
[23] Phil 2.5/8

Chapter 4
[24] Walden by Henry David Thoreau Ch 1, p8 1966, originally published 1854
[25] Rev John Notman, Newsong Community Church Bromsgrove 11.01.2015
[26] Prov 16.19
[27] Prov 22.4
[28] Micah 6.8
[29] Rev 3.17
[30] Rev 3.1 (Parenthesis mine)
[31] Matt 4.17
[32] 2 Cor 4.18
[33] John 1.12
[34] Matt 6.33 NIVUK

Chapter 5
[35] 1 Cor 5.1-2 NIVUK
[36] Rom 7.24-25
[37] John 16.13
[38] Isa 6.5
[39] Matt 7.3
[40] Matt 7.5
[41] 1 John 4.19 (Parenthesis mine)
[42] Rom 12.1
[43] Rom 12.2
[44] Jer 8.10-12 NIVUK
[45] Matt 6.31-33
[46] Isa 61.1-3
[47] 2 Cor 1.3-4 NIVUK
[48] 2 Cor 1.4 NIVUK

Chapter 6
[49] Gal 5.23 AV
[50] Matt 26.39
[51] Isa 53.7 (Parenthesis mine)
[52] Num 12.3
[53] Matt 11.29
[54] Phil2.3-8
[55] Gal 2.20
[56] Rom 6.3-4
[57] I'm not mad at God. Bethany Fellowship 1967 p26
[58] 2 Cor 5.17
[59] Luke 9.23
[60] Phil 4.11
[61] Col 3.12 AKJV
[62] 1 Tim 6.11 AKJV
[63] Titus 3.2 AKJV
[64] 1 Pet 1.3-4
[65] Ps 37.11,22,29,34
[66] 1 Pet 1.4
[67] 2 Pet 3.10; Rev 21.1
[68] 2 Pet 3.13
[69] Ps 37.11/22
[70] Eph 1.18
[71] Col 1.12
[72] Acts 17.28

Chapter 7
[73] Ps 42.1-2
[74] Ps 63.1
[75] Isa 55.1-3a
[76] Matt 6.33
[77] Deut 4.29; Jer 29.13
[78] Luke 3.38

[79] John 1.12
[80] 1 Cor 10.4
[81] John 4.13-14
[82] John 6.35
[83] John 6.51
[84] John 1.4
[85] Matt 26.26-28
[86] John 6.53-58
[87] John 6.60,66
[88] 2 Kings 4.3
[89] 2 Kings 4.6
[90] 2 Kings 13.19
[91] Luke 6.38

Chapter 8
[92] Acts 17.28
[93] James M. Gray 1905
[94] John 8.7
[95] Matt 5.38
[96] James 2.13
[97] I Cor 8.7 NIVUK
[98] 1 Cor 8.5
[99] 1 Cor 8.4
[100] 1 Cor 8.9
[101] 1 Cor 8.11-12
[102] Gal 6.1
[103] Gal 6.1
[104] Ps 103.3,8,10 (emphasis mine)
[105] Matt 6.12 NLT
[106] James 2.13
[107] Matt 13.12; 25.29
[108] Luke 6.37-38
[109] Acts 20.35
[110] Oswald Allen 1816-78 Hymns of the Christian Life (London:Nisbet 1861) p102

Chapter 10
[111] Jer 17.9 NKJV
[112] Matt 15.19-20
[113] Matt 8.2
[114] 2 Kings 17.33
[115] Luke 16.13
[116] 1 Cor 10.21
[117] James 3.9-10
[118] James 3 11-12
[119] James 4.8
[120] James 3.10
[121] Ps 24.3-4
[122] 1 John 3.1-2
[123] 1 John 3.3

[124] Phil. 2.13
[125] Theodore Monod (1836-1921)
[126] Heb 12.5-6 [Quoting Prov 3.11-12]
[127] Job 23.10
[128] Acts 15.9
[129] 1 Pet 1.22 NIVUK
[130] Heb 11.6
[131] Ps 19.1
[132] Ps 29.2
[133] Ex 40.34
[134] 2 Chon 7.1-2
[135] John 5.19, 30, 8.26-28, 12.49-50, 14.10
[136] 2 Cor 3.8-9
[137] 2 Cor 3.18
[138] Rom 3.23
[139] Brian Doerksen 2008

Chapter 11
[140] Judges 6.23-24
[141] Isa 9.6
[142] Rom 15.33, Heb 13.20
[143] Heb 7.2
[144] Job 22.21 NIVUK
[145] Ps 85.10
[146] Isa 26.3
[147] Isa 32.17 NIVUK
[148] Isa 53.5
[149] John 14.27
[150] Rom 8.6
[151] Gal 5.22
[152] Col 3.15
[153] Rom 5.1
[154] 2 Cor 5.17-18 (emphasis mine)
[155] Phil 4.6-7
[156] Phil 4.12-13
[157] Luke 10.25-37
[158] Gal 6.2
[159] Rom 12.15
[160] 1 Thess 3.12
[161] Matt 25.40
[162] Rom 8.15
[163] Rom 8.14
[164] 1 John 3.1-2
[165] John 13.35
[166] Acts 4.13 NIVUK
[167] James 3.18 NIVUK

Chapter 12
[168] Ps 119.86

[169] John 15.20
[170] 2 Tim 3.12
[171] Heb 11.36-38
[172] Miller's Church History: Pickering & Inglis 1963 various p122-181
[173] Heb 11.24-25
[174] Dan 3.16-18
[175] 2 Cor 11.23-27 NIVUK
[176] 1 Cor 4.12-13 NIVUK
[177] 2 Cor 4.8-9 NIVUK
[178] Matt 6.19-20
[179] Heb 10.34
[180] Heb 11.26 NIVUK
[181] 2 Cor 4.10 NIVUK
[182] Heb 12.2
[183] Rom 8.17 NIVUK (emphasis mine)
[184] Acts 7.55-56
[185] Acts 6.8

Chapter 13
[186] See Gen 9.15; Ex 2.24; Lev26.45; Num 10.9; Eze 16.60 as examples
[187] See Ex 3.15; Deut 5.15; 1 Chron 16.12; Neh 4.14; Ec 12.1; 2 Tim 2.8 as examples
[188] Ps 24.3
[189] Ps 24.4-6
[190] Heb 12.1-2

www.ingramcontent.com/pod-product-compliance
Lightning Source LLC
Chambersburg PA
CBHW012101050426
42443CB00030BA/3497